DOCUMENT DESIGN AND WRITING FOR YOUR ACADEMIC CAREER

Designed for graduate classroom and professional development use, this guide encourages readers to think rhetorically about audience, genre, and beyond, and to apply these reflections in meaningful ways as they craft the documents they will need throughout their careers.

The first part addresses key concepts in design convergence: design thinking, information architecture, and technology, and the second section provides application opportunities for readers. In establishing a foundational understanding of the key concepts used in design convergence, the guide brings together a range of disciplinary knowledge and experiences, including ways to work with generative artificial intelligence. Integrated into each chapter are exercises and scenarios based on real-world academic professionals' experiences that are designed to help readers deepen their understanding and consider possibilities and opportunities for (re)design in their field. Each chapter includes activities that position readers to work with their own information and content toward purposes that meet their personalized needs. These exercises include generating documents related to educating, leading, branding, and serving, such as classroom, research, and professional development materials.

Providing an equitable foundation for document genre construction and demystifying audience expectations, this book appeals to graduate students, faculty, and institutional leaders in Rhetoric, Composition, and Writing Studies as well as the humanities, arts, and social sciences.

Claire Lutkewitte is a Professor at Nova Southeastern University, USA. She is the author of *Writing in a Technological World* (Routledge, 2019).

Juliette C. Kitchens is a Professor at Nova Southeastern University, USA.

DOCUMENT DESIGN AND WRITING FOR YOUR ACADEMIC CAREER

Rhetorical Insights on Design Convergence

Claire Lutkewitte and Juliette C. Kitchens

Routledge
Taylor & Francis Group
NEW YORK AND LONDON

Designed cover image: created in Adobe Illustrator

First published 2026
by Routledge
605 Third Avenue, New York, NY 10158

and by Routledge
4 Park Square, Milton Park, Abingdon, Oxon, OX14 4RN

Routledge is an imprint of the Taylor & Francis Group, an informa business

ISBN: 978-1-041-20617-0 (hbk)
ISBN: 978-1-041-20616-3 (pbk)
ISBN: 978-1-003-71723-2 (ebk)

DOI: 10.4324/9781003717232

Typeset in Sabon
by SPi Technologies India Pvt Ltd (Straive)

CONTENTS

AUTHOR BIOGRAPHIES

Claire Lutkewitte is a Professor at Nova Southeastern University, USA. She is the author of *Writing in a Technological World* (Routledge, 2019).

Juliette C. Kitchens is a Professor at Nova Southeastern University, USA.

INTRODUCTION

As long-time Rhetoric, Composition, and Writing Studies (RCWS) academic professionals, we have been tasked countless times with creating documents that serve diverse and sometimes polyvalent purposes. Across these situations, we (Juliette and Claire) have worked equally and inextricably with content, audience, and design. Over the years, the two of us have also dedicated our time to sharing what we have learned from our studies, scholarship, and practice of design. We have done this through our research, through mentoring faculty, and through teaching graduate students how to succeed in the writing we're called to do throughout our careers as academics and professional communicators.

University faculty write often, regardless of their discipline. Faculty beyond RCWS write just as much as faculty in RCWS, and they write a variety of documents, too: from job portfolio documents to grant proposals to white papers to curriculum assessments. Yet, as we learned over the years, many faculty were never taught in graduate school how to write in these genres or craft these kinds of documents in ways that best serve their needs. When it came time in their careers to write them, they were left to find examples on their own and/or learn through trial and error. In those moments, they would have benefited from having a resource that walked them through design processes, offered examples and tips, and allowed them to explore aspects of genre and audience expectations in meaningful ways, one that offered opportunities for reflection, revision, and reinvention. This book does just that.

RCWS has a well-established scholarly history exploring the interdependence of the many facets that successful writing involves. For example,

DOI: 10.4324/9781003717232-1

one such facet, the user experience, has taught us how to effectively develop, critique, and teach our readers in a variety of situations (as a sample selection, we recommend New London Group, 1996; Kress, 2010; Wysocki and Lynch, 2017; Maimon and Peritz, 2002; Maimon and Yancey, 2024; Yancey, 2009; Shipka, 2011; Rule, 2019, 2020). Yet, while we draw on RCWS's history, this book can help graduate students and faculty throughout the arts, humanities, and social sciences develop practices (and thus documents) that account for the many professional situations that they will likely encounter in their careers.

You, our reader, may be a graduate student studying to become a sociology professor, or you may be a new history instructor, balancing your teaching load with other professional responsibilities. Regardless, the approach to document design that we provide in the following pages is reflexive and responsive, taking into consideration the message, its delivery, and its constraints, while also identifying potential sites of genre resistance and creative change. In other words, our approach in this book for document design is rhetorical in nature, one that anyone can use.

Indeed, throughout this book, we encourage you to think rhetorically about audience, genre, purpose, and beyond, and to apply these reflections in meaningful ways as you craft your documents. After all, the documents you write as faculty tell your stories and the stories of your work. They are your accounts of who you are, what you do, and what you believe. They serve you too. They can help you articulate the work you do, help you reach your career goals, and help you advocate for more equitable practices.

Documents are not neutral, fixed things. They are shaped by social, cultural, and institutional histories and the people who request them, use them, and write them. Every document you write, be it a CV or syllabus or program brochure, carries with it assumptions about whose voice matters and what counts as knowledge. Ignoring these histories ensures perpetuating exclusionary practices. Documents serve as meaning-making devices, and for faculty, this means they are more than simply records of our work and our institutions. We use documents to convey our identities, share our labor, make known our beliefs about learning, and advocate for ourselves and others. Framing documents as meaning-making devices shows us possibilities for what can be and that we have powerful and ethical decisions to make as we design and revise them.

As a reader, you may seem skeptical about our optimism given your institutional context. Perhaps, your institution's constraints make changing your documents' content or design difficult. The forms or applications you must fill out are fixed and have been for some time. Maybe the procedures you must follow for writing a curriculum proposal or syllabus have rigid rules. Maybe your administration insists that you submit documents using an online platform that only accepts a particular kind of file. This book does not guarantee it will eliminate these constraints for you. It does, however, recognize these realities and offer approaches for working within them purposively so that you can intentionally navigate them and, more importantly, challenge them. This means making informed choices through reflection and revision. It means adapting ethically and reimagining creatively. Design is an ongoing iterative process, one that extends beyond the page.

Throughout this book, you will find keywords in bold that are important to the design process and development of your professional documents. These terms are defined in the glossary, and their role in document design and design processes is developed in the chapters of this text. Some terms may carry disciplinary meaning and be familiar to you, while other terms may carry a history unfamiliar to you. They may be newly applicable to the work you are doing, may present new considerations or perspectives, or may even be fraught with negative connotations or exclusionary practices. As you will come to find in the pages that follow, reflecting on these terms can help you think deeply and widely about your beliefs about your profession, your work in it, and your writing. As you develop your design practices, you may find that some of these concepts empower creative design choices. Likewise, you may uncover inequitable genre expectations, outmoded design restrictions, or obsolete naming conventions. As you engage this book, we hope you will reflect on your own usages of terms and definitions and reshape them to be inclusive of contemporary practices and your discipline. We hope you will seek out connections to your field's past and learn its stories and, perhaps more importantly, counterstories.

I.1 Human Work: The Self and Reflection

We believe designing documents begins with rhetoric and, more specifically, understanding our role as humans in that process. However, it should be noted that in the 1990s, RCWS acknowledged that process isn't a fixed approach; it varies from person to person, situation to situation, and purpose to purpose. Recognizing that writing, more precisely composing, is a socially situated, interpretive act, RCWS developed its theory of **post-process** composing to account for the cultural and political contexts in which we write. With post-process, we came to understand that there is no formula that applies to all acts of writing; each act is connected to its context and its environment. Using reflection, for instance, is important to this understanding as it demands that writers acknowledge diverse people and contexts.

RCWS scholars have spent hundreds of years studying the benefits of reflection. Today, reflection is even built into many of our learning outcomes for our writing courses. We not only study it but teach it and use it too. Therefore, as you think rhetorically about your writing, this book will encourage you to use reflection and will provide you strategies for doing so.

The RCWS field's focus on reflection was born from the rhetorical traditions of ancient Greece and Rome. During this time, oratory was known as a noble pursuit, one requiring adept communication skills. It was from this context that rhetoricians, like Aristotle, defined the rhetorical situation, or put simply, situations that involved communication, as finding all the available means to persuade in a particular situation. His reliance on the terms *ethos*, *pathos*, *logos*, *telos*, and *kairos* helps distinguish the different strategies one could use to build a successful text. Each one of these terms necessitates reflection. Since ancient times, RCWS scholars have redeveloped these terms, applying them to mean roughly the following:

TABLE I.1 Rhetorical Situation Defined

Ethos	Writer/speaker
Pathos	Audience
Logos	Text
Telos	Purpose
Kairos	Context

To be successful communicators, RCWS scholars have argued, requires dedicated reflection on the rhetorical situation, understanding each element and how each works with the others. In other words, writers/speakers need to understand themselves as writers/speakers, have the self-awareness of their own knowledge and abilities, what they are and are not capable of, what their relationship is to the audience and to the subject matter, as well as their situatedness. It also demands writers/speakers know their purpose for communicating, their audiences, and what kind of text is most suitable to these audiences and their subject matter. Knowing the subject matter and the type of text or speech genres that the subject matter is to be communicated in is important too as is knowing the timing and place for the communications.

All of this knowing can only be achieved through reflection, not just outwardly on things like texts and audience, but inwardly on the writers/speakers themselves. This inward, personal approach to self-awareness helps a communicator grow.

Reflection is sometimes thought of as a smaller, more focused process than that of thinking itself, one that looks back on the thinker's past experiences to assess and learn from them. This, some would say, is different from thinking, which is a much broader mental process used to brainstorm ideas, solve problems, and make decisions, a process that could include reflection of the self but doesn't necessarily have to. Nor does it have to only look backward.

We believe, however, that thinking and reflecting are not different processes, but are one and the same, that you cannot do one without the other. Reflecting looks at the present, the past, and the future. It looks outward, not just inward, considering the self as well as others. Though, we argue drawing attention to how the reflection process develops self-awareness is important. This attention to the self provides a foundation for another term and strategy that we offer in this book because using the term *self* highlights the human in the writing process. In an age where technologies are at our fingertips, sometimes we fail to see just how much human work is needed to succeed in communication and in designing effective documents. RCWS scholars have always been keen on situating the human in communication. But, newer technologies, like artificial intelligence, for instance, have generated new calls in RCWS scholarship for more awareness of humans in the writing process (see Vee, 2023; Getto, Kelley, and Vance, 2025).

A **human work strategy** is rhetorical in nature but places special emphasis on the role the writer plays in the design process. One must be self-aware of the steps one takes during communication, steps that will no doubt involve tools. Tools cannot operate on their own. Humans have to design them, produce them, and use them. When we have a problem, like a design problem, we may use tools, though ultimately we are the ones who solve these problems. As you will soon see, we talk about technologies in this book as tools, specifically providing you opportunities to reflect on specific tools like artificial intelligence (AI). AI is currently a major focus for academics and is and will continue to be an important part of how and what we design moving forward. But, we argue that such a tool requires a human work strategy, one that requires a writer's self-awareness of what they are doing when using the tool. This self-awareness includes paying close attention to one's own bias and the inequities and exclusionary practices that might arise when choosing to use tools to design.

You may have heard of the **Human in the Loop (HITL) model**. When using a technology like AI, this model places humans at critical points in the problem-solving process, mainly to check whether the technology has worked effectively to solve a problem and to mitigate the technology's limitations. This model can work within a human work strategy; however, the human work strategy as proposed in this book is a strategy that prioritizes the human's contribution throughout the problem-solving process. In other words, in the HITL model, human engagement is intermittent, and in a human work strategy, human engagement is consistent throughout.

For now, many of the tools we speak of in this book, including AI, as well as all our many discussions of the self and humans point to the larger concept of this book: **convergence**, a coming together of things. Technologies are certainly the product of things coming together, but so too is rhetoric.

I.2 Convergence

Design convergence offers developing scholars and professionals ways to conceptualize what we do in order to design meaningful documents and texts that effectively communicate our work and our context(s). In part, this approach is inspired by design theory, and you may recognize several elements of this approach as you move through the text. In conversation with theories on the arrangement and flow of information, design theory promotes practices that assist us in developing versatile content structures and diverse documents that work transmedially, which in turn reflect our identities, whether it's our own professional identity, our program's institutional identity, or our field's intellectual identity.

In the title of this book, the word convergence serves as a concept that helps us think about the intersections of the work we do, how each act and thought comes together, and how we organize and circulate the information of those experiences. We use this term because, in addition to its denotative purposes, convergence spotlights the complexities and relationships of what we do on a day-to-day basis and how we represent that to others as well as how we reflect on that. The acts of writing, designing, and producing can reveal connections to us, can affirm or contest our understanding of our work and our networks, and let others know what we have achieved and what we can accomplish. As you work through this book, we hope that convergence stays with you and motivates you to bring together experience with intention and purpose.

Inherently, designing contemporary documents leverages our understanding of media convergence, a concept that grounds most of the content we encounter. For nearly twenty years, we've understood that media convergence is "the flow of content across multiple media platforms" that takes into consideration various constraints and contexts, including "the migratory behavior of media audiences" (Jenkins, 2006, p. 2). Gunther Kress (2010) identifies media convergence as a central consideration for 21st-century communication (p. 22) because it informs how we approach the organization, distribution, and reception of content. Many of us are familiar with media convergence, even if we don't explicitly acknowledge that we're engaging in practices that are shaped by it. For example, when tasked with an annual performance review, we may find it challenging to appropriately represent our work as a collection of static documents. To better communicate the work we do, we may create supplemental materials such as a professional website that integrates our teaching materials, scholarship, and evidence of our service. We may include music compositions, webinar clips, digital gallery links, or interactive maps. We likely link content from different areas of our professional experience, across different platforms and social channels, and perhaps even throughout our environments. When considering how to package the content, we brand it to create a cohesive experience for our readers. In creating this dynamic portfolio, media convergence frames our choices because, fundamentally, it is the rhetorical context through which contemporary compositions circulate.

While initially convergence remains predominantly structured as a top-down model, the [r]evolution of participatory culture and technology has shifted the power structure in some contexts, promoting convergence not just as a happening but as an analytical framework for content creation. Media convergence "manages to describe technological, industrial, cultural, and social changes, depending on who's speaking and what they think they are talking about" (Jenkins, p. 3)—it is the context in which our content lives. And, as Kress asserts, convergence "entails that occasions of and resources for knowledge production and creativity are not tied to particular sites and times" (p. 144). More simply, contemporary contexts require sustainable and adaptable methods for determining how to represent our content—design must be flexible.

The methods presented in this book use this simple concept of flexibility via an exploration of rhetorical reflection, design thinking, technology use, and information architecture to build an approach to document design that aligns with our contemporary composing environments and circulation channels while remaining individualized and adaptable. As you will see, for instance, our approach practices design thinking in ways that prioritize access through empathy while laterally problem-solving constraints. In Chapter 3, as another example, we articulate the importance of information architecture throughout the design process and identify ways to enhance information access for your audience. Convergence helps us critically narrow our design options when confronted with an array of ideas.

Integrating rhetorical reflection, design thinking, technology use, and information architecture facilitates a broad range of (re)active approaches to document design, approaches that acknowledge rapid developments within our working, writing, and composing environments. We believe that contemporary document design functions best at the borders of genre expectations, where familiarity intersects with industry and technological developments, audience needs, and cultural shifts.

More bluntly, successful contemporary document design is convergent. Along these borders, we can challenge inequitable practices and intentionally create inclusive information structures. Because we cannot know what changes are on the horizon, many of the activities in this book do not detail "proper" design but instead encourage you to pioneer new ways of knowing and sharing information, new ways of designing documents. We hope you will see this text as an illustration of the ways in which we negotiate between and among field-determined approaches and user-created approaches in document designs.

I.3 Structure

As we discuss and engage some of the various types of documents that you'll be tasked with developing over the course of your professional academic career, note that the examples we've selected for this book are not meant to be prescriptive or limiting. As you will come to find, every time you write will be different from previous experiences. Our goal in pointing this out is twofold: to help you enhance your approaches to design and to promote liberatory and rigorous information practices. To accomplish these goals, this book offers a foundation for document design that facilitates equitable, inclusive composing practices and a series of dynamic, real-world scenarios and exercises that facilitate critical engagement in those design practices. Academic professionals in a range of fields, especially those related to the arts, humanities, and social sciences, will likely find them familiar and applicable.

The book also seeks to consider changing needs within academia that reflect our technological, environmental, sociocultural, and political landscapes. Convergence is as much about the content we create as it is the context in which we live and work. Importantly, while we offer some theoretical foundation to help shape the design methods, this book is less about theorizing and more about doing. We offer strategies for conceptualizing the work you're designing, but our focus is centered on practical approaches to the everyday (and not so everyday) documents we create, share, and use as practitioners, and how we can better leverage both linear and lateral thinking in our composing processes to best represent ourselves and the work we do.

We developed the ideas grounding this book when we realized that, even as professors firmly in our second decade of professional work, we are still tasked with problem-solving document creation. We consistently work to design content that could be a part of an array of documents, and we strive to design documents that can serve multiple purposes while leveraging current technologies and affordances.

The book is divided into two parts. Although each part tackles a different part of the design process, design is a recursive process, and you may find that you have to move back and forth between the two parts as you work on revising your designs. Part I focuses on the beginning of your design task; that is, it starts with problem-solving your writing situation, making sure that you think rhetorically about your approach to creating a document that works for you and your audience. Part II moves you from the exploration of all possible pathways for your design to choosing and then drafting the best option. More specifically, you go from divergent to convergent design practices.

All in all, this book provides you with overviews of design concepts and structures and opportunities to engage in lateral thinking to problem-solve the work you're doing through a range of activities. The lateral thinking activities include scenarios and remixes. Scenarios are designed to offer a "rough sketch" rather than a detailed experience in which you can practice design techniques and approaches. Remix activities invite you to reimagine, rework, and respond—encouraging fresh perspectives, creative experimentation, and thoughtful engagement with ideas and practices. Together, these elements will help you create the documents you will use throughout your career.

At the end of each chapter, you'll find a summary of key points. The goal is to use these quick reminders as you advance through the text and to reflect on these statements as you develop your documents. This book concludes with additional scenarios to provide further opportunities to apply the concepts you're learning as you develop your design processes. We encourage you to develop your own scenarios and to work with colleagues to identify key experiences and genres applicable to your everyday work.

One of the implicit arguments we make throughout this book is that the ways in which we classify our work are becoming outmoded. As a professional member of the academic community, you're likely familiar with the tetrad of teaching, research, service, and administration. These traditional categories work well enough to encapsulate most of our traditional professional products—a syllabus is a record of our teaching, a publication is a record of our research or scholarship, our participation on a committee is evidence of service. However, we argue that our work—the everyday actions in our professional lives—more closely aligns with four points of engagement: educating, leading, branding, and serving. Is teaching not also service and leadership? What is research if it does not educate and serve? Notably, our work is rarely isolated to a single category or point. If you've ever written a cover letter, crafted a narrative for a performance review, or organized a curriculum vita, you likely experienced the struggle many of us face as we attempt to delineate our work and our actions. The lateral thinking activities reflect the traditional categories but encourage you to design in ways that relate to the four points of engagement.

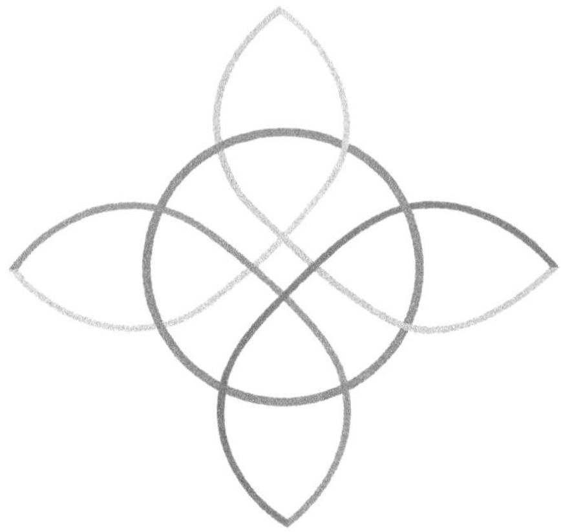

For most of us, our work overlaps among the kinds of activities we've included and the points of engagement you'll find us referencing in the book. Our aim is to avoid hierarchically ordering or linearly constructing these and to encourage you to find ways to design documents that problem-solve the issues we face within academia and as practitioners engaged in acts of composing. To visually represent this approach to successfully crafting documents, we use the quaternary knot, shown on this book's cover, composed of four brackets and a circle. The four brackets represent the foundation of this book: 1) rhetorical reflection, 2) design thinking, 3) technology use, and 4) information architecture. The circle represents convergence. As Deutsch (2017) writes, "...convergence is marked by a blurring of lines, disciplines, and roles brought about by interdisciplinary collaboration" (p. 5). Rhetorical reflection, design thinking, technology use, and information architecture are not exclusive of one another, and they are not grounded in a single discipline; they are intertwined, integrated, and interdisciplinary. The convergence of these things is what produces your documents successfully. Thus, not all will have their own separate chapter. For example, while we have introduced the concept of rhetorical reflection in this introduction as a process that involves reflection on the self, purpose, audience, text, and context, it is a concept you will see entangled throughout the book. Likewise, design thinking, technology use, and information architecture are singularly tools—processes and platforms we engage daily—but rarely are we called upon to use them individually. More often, as we craft and produce documents, we draw on these collectively to facilitate content and design. That is why we see rhetorical reflection, design thinking, technology use, and information architecture more as a tangled knot; when used together, they are strong.

To put this another way, the symbol of the quaternary knot on this book's cover is a simplified version of this illustration of convergent design's quadrants. This illustration includes the entanglements you will explore in this book. Because there are many entanglements, we choose instead to use the quaternary knot as the symbol we hope you will associate with the design concepts brought together in this book. The quaternary knot that you see on the cover, with its entangled lines and precise edges, its vibrant colors, and its unity in shape, is something we hope you will find easier to visualize as a symbol of design convergence.

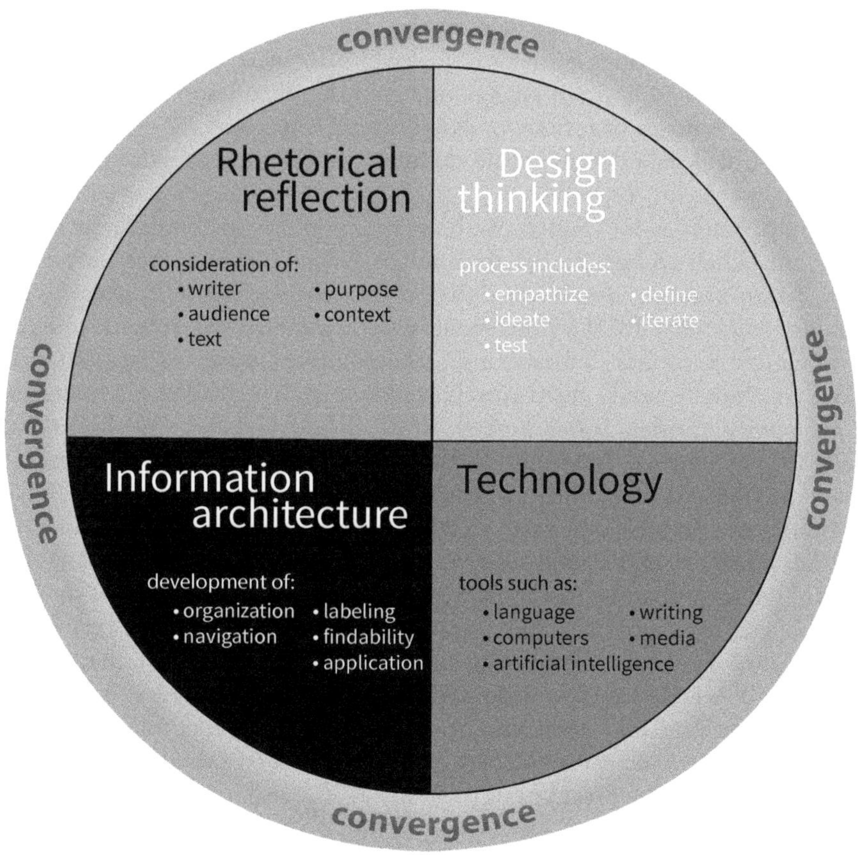

Map of convergent design's quadrants.

In each chapter, you'll see scenarios grounded in contemporary academic professionals' lived experiences that present work as having entangled elements we often have to negotiate and balance as we design and construct documents. We hope that you will keep the image of the quaternary knot in mind as you work through these scenarios. Indeed, the scenarios position you to problem-solve design and information architecture issues in an effort to address the complexities and challenges we face while actively crafting documents in our busy lives. In each part of this book, you'll also find activities that encourage you to move beyond the screen or page to find connections with your material and lived reality. These activities work well with the scenarios to provide a deeper, more meaningful approach to design thinking.

As composing practitioners, we are skilled in thinking rhetorically about the purposes and audiences for our writing. **Documents**—a term used throughout this text to denote the various kinds of products we craft and circulate—serve a multitude of purposes. We craft documents to communicate our scholarship, garner professional placement and advancements, articulate curriculum, and engage our communities. Importantly, we use these documents to negotiate, to assess, and to represent.

As you will see in many of the chapters, we offer instances of reflection and action meant for you to push back and create moments of advocacy and opportunities for change. We hope that you use this book to advocate on your behalf and on the behalf of others when you encounter exclusionary design practices and institutional norms that are not reflective of who we are as faculty. RCWS practitioners are acutely aware of the inequities in languages, modes, and writing technologies because we have studied and continue to study them closely. Indeed, we have called for linguistic sovereignty (Lyons, 2000; Powell, 2002; King, Gubele, and Anderson, 2015), social justice (Inoue, 2019; McCabe and Juszkiewicz, 2023; Lockett et al., 2021), and body equity (Brueggemann et al., 2001; Price, 2011; Muhlhauser, Krauss, Sheffield, 2022), and we continue, as practitioners and as a field, to maintain these priorities in our work and our scholarship. Thus, we hope that the methods presented here carry on this tradition and enable you to identify genre expectations and practices that are exclusionary or no longer relevant and engender not only rationales for change but also the development of new equitable and inclusive practices. As critical thinkers, readers, and designers, we hope this text enhances the intentionality of your own creative practices and facilitates your ability to recognize intentionality in the practices of others.

I.4 AI Use and Transparency in This Text

As you read through this book, you will see examples illustrating different uses of AI. Creating a book about document design processes in the age of AI would be incomplete without discussing AI at length and in a multitude of ways. Our discussions are bolstered by suggestions of when and how the technology can be used throughout the design process. We also included demonstrations as examples, specifically in the "What AI Has to Say" illustrations. In Chapter 2, we discuss different ways to frame AI broadly within your designing and writing processes, and more specifically in different kinds of projects you may encounter in your professional academic experience.

However, while we use large language models (LLMs), we want to acknowledge that all tools, including AI tools, have their biases, limitations, and exclusionary practices. These have been documented time and again by RCWS scholars and others. As the writers of this book, we grappled with whether to include such a technology. Witnessing how our colleagues and students engage it, however, we felt we could not ignore it in a book about designing documents.

In each chapter, you will see special boxes illustrating the output we received when we asked AI, specifically LLMs, to reflect on particular ideas. What you see in the shaded boxes is the material generated by AI from our prompts. For example, we asked ChatGPT (GPT-5) to define convergence in the context of designing documents. Here is what we got in return:

WHAT AI HAS TO SAY:

"Convergence" in document design usually refers to the way different elements (visual, textual, and structural) come together to reinforce meaning and guide readers. In other workds, it refers to the alignment and integration of multiple modes of communication (text, visuals, layout, navigation) so they work together together a unified purpose. In technical communication and writing studies, it often describes how *form and function converge* to meet audience needs. It's both a design principle and a rhetorical strategy.

Code credit: OpenAI, *ChatGPT* (2025, October 8)

Example of an output generated by the prompt: "What does convergence mean when designing documents?" Code credit: OpenAI, *ChatGPT* (2025, October 8).

We found the outputs included in these examples weren't *wrong*, but they weren't *right*, either. We proceeded with caution, read many diverse perspectives about how AI might help or hinder design, and debated among ourselves about what we wanted to say about the technology and its product (i.e., output), and how we would say it. We chose specific LLMs, not because they are perfect systems—they are not (more on this later in this book)—but because these are the most popular tools at the time we are writing this text. We hope you read our "What AI Has to Say" sections critically and cautiously and ask questions of them like we have. We mean for this to be another moment for reflection in this book, one in which you are asked to weigh information, consider how it is designed and shared, and identify how its use can be improved upon. To help you in this endeavor, we provide our own critiques and questions. The following image reflects our critiquing and questioning:

WHAT AI HAS TO SAY:

"Convergence" in document design usually refers to the way different elements (visual, textual, and structural) come together to reinforce meaning and guide readers. In other workds, it refers to the alignment and integration of multiple modes of communication (text, visuals, layout, navigation) so they work together together a unified purpose. In technical communication and writing studies, it often describes how *form and function converge* to meet audience needs. It's both a design principle and a rhetorical strategy.

Code credit: OpenAI, *ChatGPT* (2025, October 8)

This is oversimplified and assumes that a discipline has one stable definition. It does not consider alternative frameworks.

This assumes what an audience needs, but who is the audience? Does this audience include everyone? Can everyone access this definition?

Defining this as a principle implies that this is a neutral or standard definition. We know that concepts are culturally constructed. Whose culture does this definition represent?

Example of Claire and Juliette's response to the output generated by the prompt: "What does convergence mean when designing documents?" Code credit: OpenAI, *ChatGPT* (2025, October 8).

We've also included additional discussion of these examples in the chapters' text. We hope that you will grapple with tough questions as you work with AI. Asking "What is lost when we rely on AI to do some of the work for us?" is an ethical questions that we need to think about often. For example, we might use AI to help us do and write our research, to summarize the sources we found, for instance. We must think about what we are missing when we read summaries instead of whole texts. How does this ultimately change our writing? Do we get the true essence of the source, or does that even matter if we can still achieve our purpose? Writing shapes us, and so too do the technologies we use to do this writing. As you work through this book, we encourage you to think critically and deeply about how writing technologies like AI shape you as a thinker, learner, and writer.

Finally, while we use and encourage you to use AI guardedly, we also do not want to perpetuate the idea that writing is something that has to be done efficiently and as quickly as possible. In other words, to get it out of the way as fast as possible so that you can do more important things. Writing is important, and we do not wish for AI to tell us otherwise.

References

Brueggemann, Brenda Jo, White, Linda Feldmeier, Dunn, Patricia A., Heifferon, Barbara A., & Cheu, Johnson. (2001). Becoming visible: Lessons in disability. *College Composition and Communication 52*(3), 368–398.

Deutsch, Randy. (2017). *Convergence: The redesign of design*. Wiley.

Getto, Guiseppe, Kelley, Susan, & Vance, Bremen. (2025). How to write with GenAI: A framework for using generative AI to automate writing tasks in technical communication. *Journal of Technical Writing and Communication*, https://doi.org/10.1177/00472816251332208.

Inoue, Asao. (2019). How do we language so people stop killing each other, or what do we do about white language supremacy. *College Composition and Communication*, *71*(2), 352–369.

Jenkins, Henry. (2006). *Convergence culture*. New York University Press. https://archive.org/details/isbn_9780814742815

King, Lisa, Gubele, Rose, & Anderson, Joyce Rain (Eds.). (2015). *Survivance, sovereignty, and story: Teaching American Indian rhetorics*. Utah State University Press.

Kress, Gunther. (2010). *Multimodality: A social semiotic approach to contemporary communication*. Routledge.

Lockett, Alexandria, Ruiz, Iris D., Sanchez, James Chase, & Carter, Christopher. (2021). *Race, rhetoric, and research methods*. WAC Clearinghouse; University Press of Colorado.

Lyons, Scott Richard. (2000). Rhetorical sovereignty: What do American Indians want from writing? *College Composition and Communication*, *51*(3), 447–468.

Maimon, Elaine, & Peritz, Janice. (2002). *A writer's resource*, 1st ed. McGraw-Hill.

Maimon, Elaine, & Yancey, Kathleen Blake. (2024). *A writer's resource*, 7th ed. McGraw-Hill.

McCabe, Rachel, & Juszkiewicz, Jennifer. (2023). *Composition & rhetoric in contentious times*. University Press of Colorado.

Muhlhauser, Paul, Krauss, Hannah, & Sheffield, Jenna. (2022). Imagining rhetorical equity: Thoughts on unshaming audience. *Computers and Composition Online*. http://cconlinejournal.org/unshaming/index.html.

New London Group (1996). A pedagogy of multiliteracies: Designing social futures. *Harvard Educational Review*, *66*(1). https://www.sfu.ca/~decaste/newlondon.htm

OpenAI. (2025, October 8). *ChatGPT* (GPT-5) [Large Language Model]. https://chatgpt.com

Powell, Malea. (2002). Rhetorics of survivance: How American Indians use writing. *College Composition and Communication*, *53*(3), 396–434.

Price, Margaret. (2011). *Mad at school: Rhetorics of mental disability and academic life*. University of Michigan Press.

Rule, Hannah. (2019). *Situating writing processes*. WAC Clearinghouse; University Press of Colorado. https://wac.colostate.edu/books/perspectives/situating

Rule, Hannah. (2020). Beyond page design: Writing as multimodal embodied meaning. In Pegeen Reichert Powell (Ed.), *Writing changes: Alphabetic text and multimodal composition* (pp. 62–82). MLA Press.

Shipka, Jody. (2011). *Toward a composition made whole*. University of Pittsburgh Press.

Vee, Annette. (2023). Large language models write answers. *Composition Studies*, *51*(1), 176–181.

Wysocki, Anne F., & Lynch, Dennis A. (2017). *Compose design advocate*, 3rd ed. Pearson.

Yancey, Kathleen Blake. (2009). Re-designing graduate education in composition and rhetoric: The use of remix as concept, material, and method. *Computers and Composition*, *26*(1), 4–12.

PART I

Problem-Solving the Work

1

DESIGN THINKING IN ACADEMIC DOCUMENTS

1.1 Document Design as Problem-Solving

Creating professional documents, especially as you begin your career or start a new position, can feel like an overwhelming problem to solve. We aren't always familiar with the genre expectations or the expectations of our audiences. We may be unfamiliar with an institution's context and history. We might not know what kinds of circulation or distribution constraints that exist for the document, or we may have little information about how long the document will be in use. The myriad problems we face when we're asked to produce a cover letter, a course assignment sheet, or a program report differ greatly and, as professionals in academia, we are frequently positioned to create many of these documents simultaneously.

RCWS strategies for rhetorical reflection lend themselves to problem-solving, frequently taking up issues of design in the name of invention, arrangement, style, and delivery. Arguably, for the better part of 70 years, the field has centered its focus on heuristics that can aid problem-solving in composing processes. This is most evident in the ways RCWS has incorporated creative problem-solving in writing classrooms by utilizing design thinking strategies. Specifically, Jason Chew Kit Tham's (2022) work looks at design thinking's history in relation to teaching writing in college classrooms. "Design thinking," he writes, "is a human-centered problem-solving philosophy and methodology that aims to pursue solutions or strategies to address complex social problems through an iterative design process" (p. 13). Students in his classrooms work through real-world problems using design thinking in transformative and creative ways.

DOI: 10.4324/9781003717232-3

Likewise, Scott Wible (2020) also traces the history of design thinking in RCWS and describes using design thinking as a way "to help students develop the creativity needed to meet complex challenges in their academic, civic, and professional lives" (p. 400). While both Tham and Wible tie design thinking to the college writing classroom, the concepts can be applied to how faculty approach their own writing. Highlighting both writer and audience roles in design thinking, Wible suggests that using this framework facilitates "develop[ing] innovative solutions through direct, regular engagement with people" (p. 401). Indeed, design thinking encourages writers to "inquire into the unfamiliar" in order to become "more creative problem solvers" (Wible, p. 402, 406). Building on design thinking's history, Wible shows us how students can do this by working with point-of-view statements, empathy, ideation, prototyping, and testing. What has been proven to work by Tham and Wible in the college writing classroom can also work for faculty writers.

While Tham and Wible's work is a bit more recent, RCWS's use of design thinking concepts extends back to writing scholars who thought it best to teach students that writing was not just a five-paragraph formulaic essay. Indeed, most of us know that college composition, moreover professional writing, is not that at all. RCWS scholars have transitioned the Composition classroom from the linear, text-based essays common in the 19th and 20th centuries to today's sensory-rich, multimodal compositions. As the field gradually learned to integrate image, sound, and texture throughout the 1970s, 1980s, and 1990s, we also struggled with disciplinary identity. As a result, the field embraced distinctions between academic writing, professional writing, and creative writing. Pedagogues increasingly shaped their first-year writing classrooms to prioritize logic and analysis over creativity. Creative opportunities for writing students became scarce outside of specialized courses.

At the turn of the 21st century, Geoffrey Sirc (2002) suggested that Composition had "narrow-band[ed]" itself into the "trappings of traditional academia" (p. 7) in the name of disciplinary validity and proposed redesigning Composition Studies in the spirit of "writing-as-life" (p. 8). Sirc gave voice to those who saw Composition as a discipline that was bound by surrounding expectations: disciplines that restrict writing to five-paragraph essays, grammar, and Standard Academic English despite RCWS's efforts to share our expanded composing repertoire. He argued that the way forward required looking back and encouraged practitioners to reframe Composition as a *happening*, a participatory (often avant-garde) performance that was usually part of a sequence of events occurring across multiple spaces over a specific period of time. In wrestling some of our field's grandest problems—craft and creation, disciplinary validity and institutional purpose, resistance and assimilation—Sirc leveraged a historical movement to demonstrate how we might design our work to resist the "curriculum of the academic essay" (p. 263), or the structured formalist embrace the field grounded itself in throughout the late 20th century (and arguably never fully released).

Moving in a fully different direction, a few years later Gunther Kress (2010), in *Multimodality*, theorized **design** as "prospective," an act of critically informed anticipation that prioritizes user "realization of their interest in their world" (p. 6). Importantly, Kress specifies that design departs from "anchoring communication in *convention* as social regulation" (p. 6; emphasis orig.) and "rests on the possibility of choice" (p. 28). In a more pragmatic approach to design than Sirc's, Kress centered the field's approach to design in issues of access, affordance, materiality, and purpose. Reflecting on these issues opened the door for writers (and writing scholars and teachers) to consider not just what was said in a text but what the text looked like, how it was built (beyond the words), and how it was used. From this, scholars realized there was no such thing as a text that employed just one mode as was the thinking before. Now, we had to consider how the linguistic mode (words on paper) worked with *and because of* other modes present, such as the spatial mode (spacing and placement) and the visual mode (typography and color). If we wanted to understand a genre, we had to not only look at the linguistic mode, but we needed to look at the other modes too. What makes a grant proposal a grant proposal isn't just its words; it's also how those words are arranged (spatial mode) and represented (visual mode). Without the correct use of these modes, we would have a hard time recognizing a grant proposal.

Shortly after, in *Remixing Composition*, Jason Palmeri (2012) posited that writing students and visual arts students engage in a similar "recursive process of discovery," or problem finding (p. 30). Palmeri reaches back to RCWS scholarship from the 1960s and 1970s to remind us that **multimodality** isn't new. He points out that scholars realized that technology's impact on the "field's conventional privileging of linearity and originality in print text" required expanding our understanding of composing to include "analyzing and/or producing participatory, associative texts that made meaning through juxtaposition, incorporated found images and words, and enabled audience interaction" (p. 88). Building on this, scholars such as Kathleen Yancey, Jody Shipka, Byron Hawk, Johndan Johnson-Eilola, and Stuart Selber, among others (Johnson-Eilola & Selber, 2007; Shipka, 2011), have worked to establish and explore composing as **assemblages**.

According to Yancey and McElroy (2017), assemblage is "a theory and practice located in media, context, and combinations" (p. 3). Acknowledging the complexities of assemblages—that they exist in the shared places and spaces of composers, audiences, texts, and technologies; that they challenge (and often resist) normative textual practices—contemporary RCWS scholarship establishes a balance between Sirc and Kress. Arguably, assemblages are impermanent solutions to found problems. This, we argue, is how we might frame contemporary document design.

More recent RCWS scholarship has returned to the term "**craft**" to define what we do to communicate meaning when there is a coming together of things—people, ideas, materials, technology, power. Drawing from new materialist rhetorics, Leigh Gruwell (2022) writes, "craft also understands that rhetorical action is not the product of a singular, human actor but rather a result of assemblages of varied human and nonhuman actors" (p. 6). Craft, according to Gruwell, "recognizes rhetoric as a material practice that is both structured by power and carries significant ethical weight" (p. 7).

In an effort to treat document design as a prospective process of discovery, we see each potential design as a collection of choices a human must make, a transitory response to a contextual moment. As such, we frame documents as found problems, situations with established parameters and expectations—not all of which remain applicable or appropriate for modern users—and document design as problem-solving for humans, not through a heuristic or algorithmic approach, but through a design thinking approach.

1.2 Understanding Design Thinking

At its most basic, **design thinking** encourages human-centered problem-solving. Here, human-centered means both self-centered and user-centered. It promotes a multidimensional approach to a situation or issue. Frequently, design thinking is employed to address **wicked problems**, or those which are so complex that they often elude a singular or sustainable solution. While academic professionals face wicked problems throughout their careers (Marback, 2009), learning to leverage this methodology to help us develop materials that are responsive to contemporary contexts and values can assist us in problem-solving dilemmas with various degrees of "wickedness." As Tham and Thominet note, "design thinking is a unique exploratory *lens* for problem-solving that offers a flexible, heuristic approach to innovation" (Tham, 2022, p. 3). And explore we will.

The iterative process of design thinking is not wholly unfamiliar for RCWS practitioners. Our field's rich understanding of composing processes has served us well for decades and continues to do so. Similar to the evolution of composing processes developed by RCWS researchers, the process of design thinking has also evolved to meet contemporary contextual and production needs. In doing so, design thinking allows us to build on that foundation with a process that reflects contemporary composition practices, spaces, and places. For instance, design thinking's inclusion of user experience (UX) and user interface (UI) practices alongside its prioritization of affect and cultural theories promotes analysis and experimentation that potentially produces a wide range of possibilities. Building on the work of Gunther Kress, James Purdy (2014) posits:

> Design thinking treats composing decisions as deliberate and consequential. A design thinking-influenced writing process, then, does not end with critique or analysis; it is not bound by the conventions of "past production" (Kress, "English" 87; see also Kress, *Literacy*) but analyzes in order to create. While analysis in and of itself can be generative, design thinking reinforces that analysis is often most effective as a counterpart to synthesis.
>
> *(p. 626)*

Balancing analysis and synthesis, the current process structure commonly used in design thinking evolves from the work of designers at IDEO and Stanford's d.school (n.d.) and involves five iterative stages: empathize, define, ideate, prototype, and test. Because the process is recursive, we've separated iterate as a sixth stage. Sometimes you will see iterate grouped together with the final step in the process, test, and some constructions of the design thinking framework emphasize that iteration occurs throughout the process. Just as revision is a defined stage of the writing process despite occurring throughout it, we find that iteration can happen throughout the design thinking process, even though it more frequently occurs after testing. These six stages, however, cannot begin without rhetorical reflection, specifically of your self-awareness of your situatedness in the design problem. In addition, these six stages also rely on our ability to think linearly and laterally. Thus, design thinking as a process may look visually something like this:

TABLE 1.1 Six Stages of Design Thinking

<table>
<tr><td rowspan="6">All stages require linear thinking and lateral thinking.</td><td>Empathize</td><td>Understanding your audience</td><td rowspan="6">All stages require rhetorical reflection, analysis, and synthesis.</td></tr>
<tr><td>Define</td><td>Identifying, describing, and making clear what problem you are solving</td></tr>
<tr><td>Ideate</td><td>Generating creative solutions</td></tr>
<tr><td>Prototype</td><td>Quickly developing a model</td></tr>
<tr><td>Test</td><td>Observing users use</td></tr>
<tr><td>Iterate</td><td>Revising and developing another version</td></tr>
</table>

While listed in chart form, these are not always achieved in a particular order. Sometimes, we have to move back and forth between these stages or use more than one simultaneously.

Empathizing requires developing a rich understanding of the **user** (i.e., your audience) and their user experience. It is frequently achieved through research, including observing your audience and interacting with them in ways that will help you uncover their motivations and their reactions. Empathizing requires reflection on the rhetorical situation. In better understanding the user and the situation, you can reduce or eliminate potential assumptions that could misdirect your design efforts. In the context of document design, this analytical stage may help you better understand your audience's use of a document, their emotional response to it, their preferences for accessing and navigating information contained in it, and their potential applications of the content. Some user responses to documents may be concrete (e.g., hiring committee readers will access your CV to develop a broad understanding of the scope of your experience), and some may be more abstract (e.g., hiring committee readers will access your CV to begin developing a sense of your values).

It's important in this step to gain a sense of what your audience thinks, says, feels, and does (Wible, p. 23, in Tham, 2022). One way to develop the empathy stage is to interview users or representatives who can share their experiences. Exploring the what, when, where, why, and how of the issue with your audience creates contextual dimensions that deepen your understanding of the problem or issue and often leads to a more expansive understanding of it. Many designers then map what they've uncovered in the empathy stage in order to better analyze their discovery data and visualize the complexity of the user.

Some design problems require us to include ourselves in the empathy stage. Just as we research our audience, we may need to research our own position to the problem. For example, if we are developing policy statements for a community that we are separate from, we would want to understand ourselves as part of empathizing with this audience. In these cases, reflecting on the whole rhetorical situation (the writer, audience, text, context, etc.) may serve us in developing documents that our audience will find cogent and accessible.

Defining the problem is frequently a sustained reiterative step in the design thinking process that involves identifying, describing, and making clear what the problem is. Ideally, problem definition occurs after empathizing, but you may find these occur concurrently, that you refine and reframe the problem as you develop an empathic understanding of your audience in relation to the text or issue. You are also just as likely to return to the defining stage throughout the ideate, prototype, and test stages of

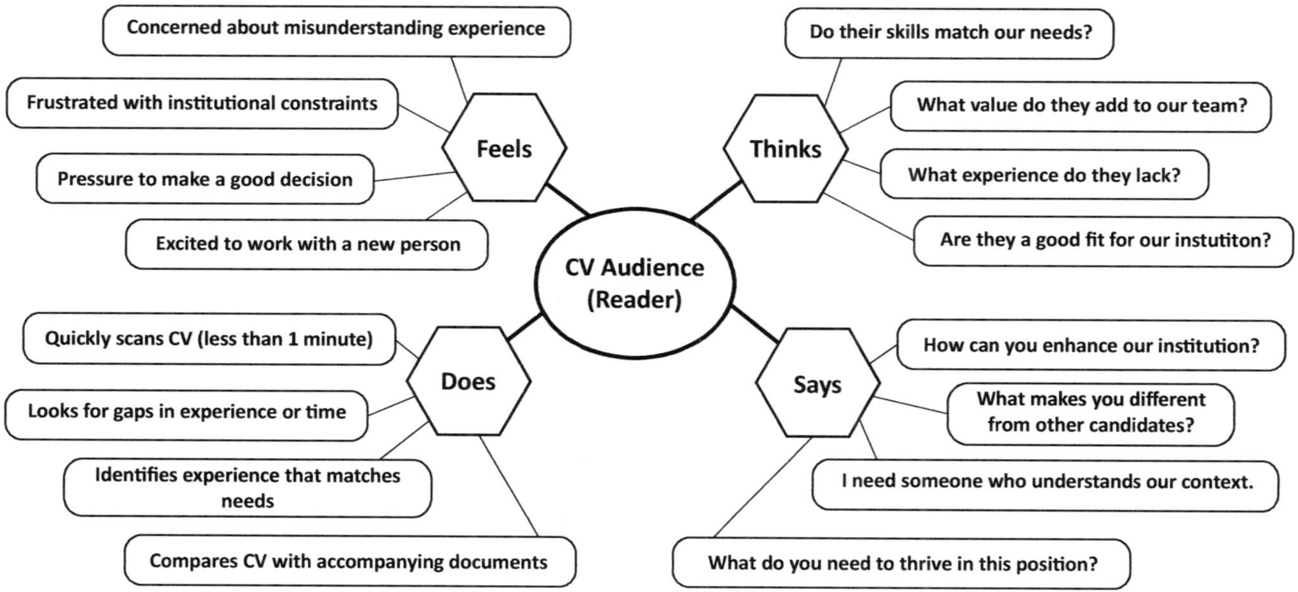

FIGURE 1.1 Empathy map.

This empathy map centers the user in order to help the designer anticipate their CV reader's experience. The primary nodes include the observed user phenomena "says" and "does," and the inferred user phenomena "feels" and "thinks," which are the standard quadrants in an empathy map. Designers ideally will return to the empathy map throughout the design process and revise it as the user(s) context changes.

the design thinking process as you uncover new knowledge and develop a better understanding of your audience's need(s) and your document's context.

Problem definitions should be focused, clear, and insightful. Most design theorists agree that successful definitions are generally concise and encourage **point-of-view (PoV) statements.** PoV statements, which are similar to problem statements, include the user (audience), need (problem/purpose), and insight (information gathered in the empathy stage). Each of these categories begins with the empathy stage, and each is developed by continually synthesizing the information discovered through analysis at different stages of the process. One way to conceptualize the difference between a problem statement and a PoV statement is that problem statements often center the object, or thing, within the problem. PoV statements center the subject, or user, and their need in relation to the problem. Defining the problem (i.e., a problem definition) and creating a PoV statement are sometimes treated as synonymous, but we find it helpful to craft the problem definition more broadly and then generate the PoV statement from the definition.

If you were a graduate student designing your CV but had limited experiences in the classroom, here would be a good example of a problem definition for such a situation:

> *As a graduate student, my limited teaching experience overshadows the range of skills I've developed through different kinds of classroom opportunities. I need to spotlight my skills and abilities so that hiring committees can quickly assess my readiness for the job.*

You could then turn this problem definition into a PoV statement by working through it in the following worksheet:

TABLE 1.2 PoV Worksheet

User	*Need*	*Insight*
Hiring committee readers	Quickly identify in my CV document my diverse teaching skills	• Readers often have a large number of CVs to review in the hiring process and therefore can't spend too much time with any one document. • Teaching is central to all faculty hiring positions and also indicates a range of durable skills that could be of interest to nonacademic hiring committees, too.

Now, you could take this worksheet and turn it into a PoV statement that centers the user and includes both the primary need and insight gathered in the empathy stage:

PoV Statement	*Hiring committee readers need to quickly identify my diverse teaching skills because teaching is central to all faculty hires and readers have limited time to spend with each application.*

This PoV statement then becomes a starting point for designing the CV. This statement indicates that you need to prioritize the skills over the range of experience. You might frame your experience through identifiable skills instead of courses taught. For example, a standard approach in CV design for teaching experience might look like:

TEACHING EXPERIENCE

COURSES, INSTRUCTOR OF RECORD

COMP 2000 Advanced College Writing — Spring 2026, 1 section
COMP 1500 College Writing — Fall 2025, 1 section

Example of a CV section addressing teaching experience.

This design clearly communicates that you've taught two courses but doesn't indicate specific skills you've acquired or illustrate the breadth of your experience, which is your goal. You might revise this design to something like:

PEDAGOGICAL EXPERIENCE

COMPETENCIES

Lesson planning
Assessment
Collaboration
Individual instruction
Multimodal instruction

COURSES, INSTRUCTOR OF RECORD

COMP 2000 Advanced College Writing — Spring 2026, 1 section
COMP 1500 College Writing — Fall 2025, 1 section

TUTORING

Writing and Communication Center — 2023-2025
Administrative Coordinator (tutor education, center communication; Tutor; Study Group Leader (BIOL 1200, PSYC 1450)

GRADUATE COURSEWORK

WRIT 5100 Teaching Writing
WRIT 5150 Teaching Writing Online
WRIT 5340 Writing Center Praxis

Example of a reimagined CV section addressing pedagogical experience.

This design deviates from standard CV structure without sacrificing audience expectations and genre conventions. Hiring committees reading a CV anticipate a section addressing teaching experience; this design offers readers a more contextualized impression.

TABLE 1.3 Remix: PoV Statement

PoV statements are useful for focusing the problem, and designers often allow the PoV to guide their direction. What are some professional situations beyond document design in which a PoV statement could be helpful (e.g., developing an approach to one-to-one student meetings)? Use the space below to work on a PoV statement for other situations. How could a PoV statement promote a shared understanding or help you develop a more concrete awareness of an issue? What steps will you take to identify the "insight"?

Professional situation:

Problem definition:

User	Need	Insight

PoV Statement:

Ideation occurs throughout the design process and functions similarly to brainstorming and (early) outlining. This stage prioritizes creativity and possibility, and it frequently relies on unconventional thinking. When you're in the ideation stage, you're trying to come up with as many solutions to the problem as possible; how functional or plausible these solutions are is less important than simply letting your creativity take you into diverse generative directions. Ideation is the stage in which we try to attend to every possible user voice and experience.

Because of the range of prospective approaches, content, or applications uncovered in the ideation stage, not every possible solution or approach developed in ideation will be novel, but it's important to find ways to avoid judgment in this stage. Ideation, after all, is about *possibility*, as in finding all the available means, as Aristotle would say. You'll analyze the value and relevance of the ideas somewhat, but more thoroughly later; in this stage, you just want to get ideas out.

To engage this stage, you might map or storyboard your ideas, as you see in the two examples provided in Figures 1.2 and 1.3. You might seek out another person or small group of people with whom you can discuss ideas, play with keywords or concepts, or even role-play to generate ideas. You might doodle images or gamestorm. The best way to ideate is somewhat dependent on you and the context in which you're working. For example,

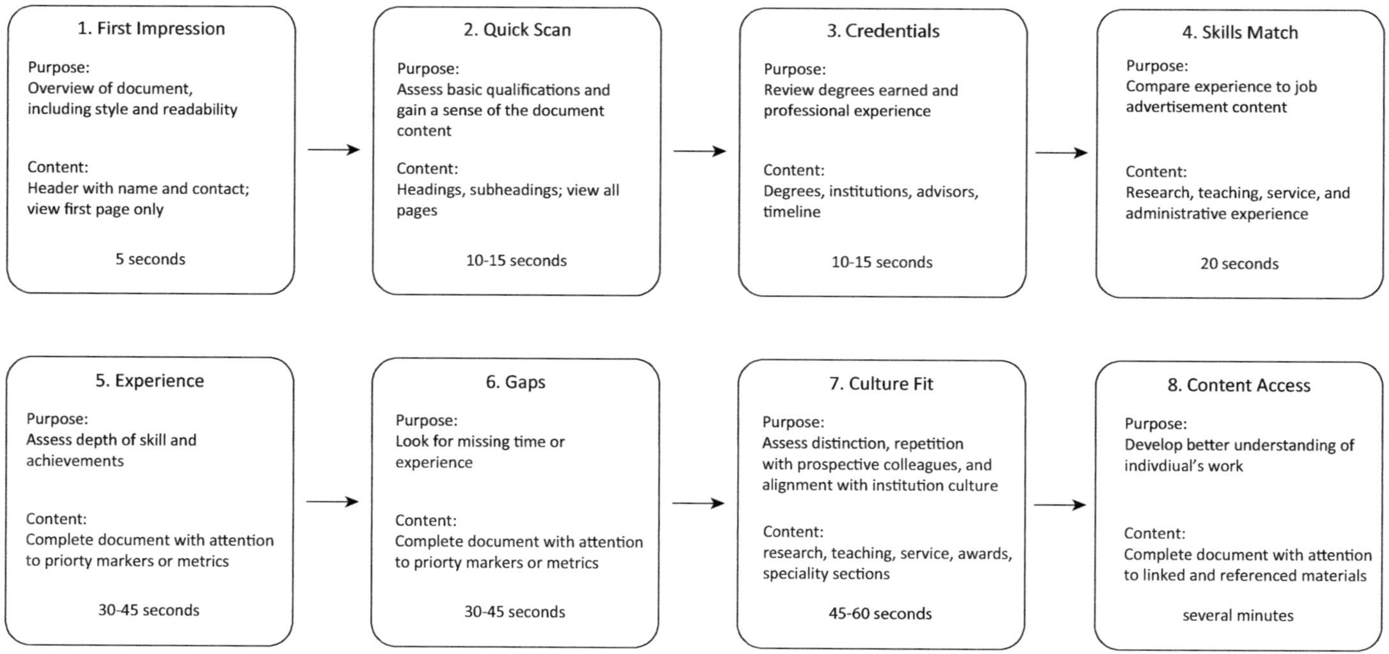

FIGURE 1.2 CV review storyboard.

This is an example of a CV storyboard that anticipates the reader experience. Each frame mirrors the priorities of the user and how much time the user will likely spend at each step of the review. This helps the designer establish the elements of the CV that will speak to each priority.

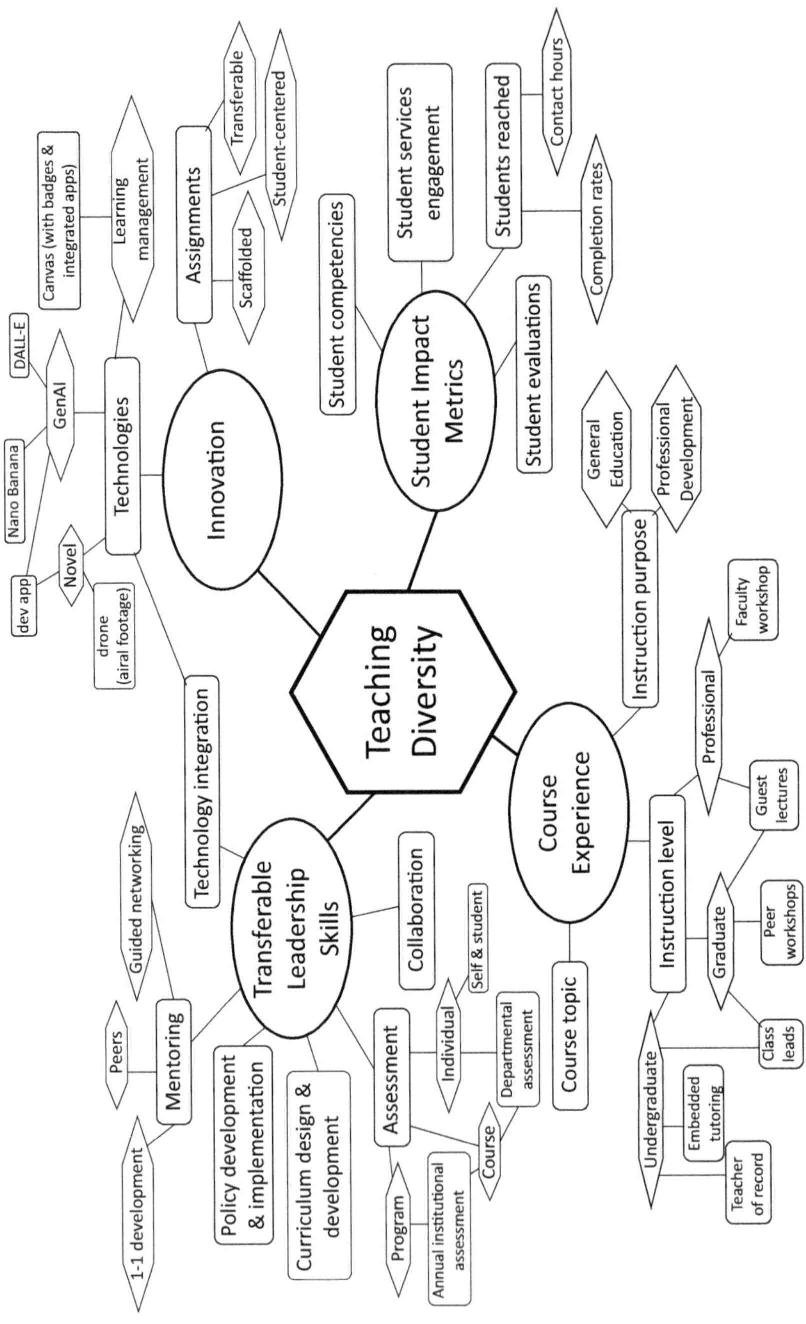

FIGURE 1.3 CV development brainstorm.

This is an example of a brainstorm map for a CV that focuses specifically on the problem of spotlighting traditional and nontraditional teaching experiences so that readers can quickly capture the range of the designer's pedagogical activity.

Claire sees herself as a pragmatic thinker and feels she gets more out of analytical exercises. When working through a design problem, she inevitably gets a sheet of paper or finds a whiteboard that she can begin drawing on. Using the space for storyboarding, much like the example in Figure 1.2, provides Claire with a somewhat linear map of possibilities. Juliette, on the other hand, tends to doodle ideas in various spaces and likes to gamify brainstorming through activities like timed sprints, word associations, and role-playing.

The next two stages, **prototyping** and **testing**, are somewhat entangled. If you're familiar with the writing process, you might conceptualize these as aligning with drafting and revising. While some similarities exist (see Purdy for an excellent discussion of the parallels between design thinking and the writing process), the differences warrant deeper discussion. Drafting and revising, for most of us, take time. We often spend days, weeks, or even months thinking about the content, writing it, and perfecting it. This process looks different for everyone, and while some of us might share our work throughout the process, others might not share the content until the draft is complete, if at all. If we share our draft with the intent to gather feedback, we may or may not integrate those suggestions into our work. Prototyping, often referred to as *rapid prototyping*, involves quickly developing a model, introducing the model to users to *test*, observing and guiding the user interface, and revising the model to enhance the user experience. Translating this to drafting a document: we would quickly sketch our ideas out, share them with an audience of potential users, gather feedback, and use that feedback to create a new, improved version of the document. Sounds similar, right? As Bradley Dilger asserts, "testing can be the engine of *iteration* that should be at the heart of design thinking" (Tham, 2022, p. 41). With design thinking, we test our work early and center the feedback in our revision.

Iteration correlates to revision as [re]vision—as a re-seeing of the prototype through the lens of discovery. It may imply that there are errors to be corrected or that the draft needs to be repaired. Certainly, there is a general sense that iterations will improve on the existing design or model, but these improvements do not necessarily correlate to broken or bad design. In some instances, iterations may permit you to enhance existing features or add new elements to a document. Iterations may be generated by analyzing feedback that uncovers new insights to your user's experiences or needs and synthesizing that information into the document's content and structure.

As with drafting and revising in the writing process, you move among the prototyping and testing stages (and sometimes these lead us back to defining or to ideation) in an effort to build on the possibilities uncovered in each. You rely on analysis and synthesis throughout these stages to determine what and how you need to reconsider, and you tinker with the model, or draft, until the design contextually meets the user's need in relation to the problem definition and/or PoV statement.

Right now, you're holding a living example of the design thinking process: this book. If we've done our job, the text likely feels like a linear production, but the process of designing it was recursive and nebulous. When we first started developing this workbook, we entered the empathy stage and conducted interviews with and observed our colleagues across the RCWS field at several institutions. In their early stages of professional development, colleagues noted they weren't sure how to create many of the documents we are tasked with generating in our careers (such as a teaching statement, a program or course proposal, an effective assignment sheet, etc.), and we often heard that there were limited resources, both textual and personal, addressing this issue. We collected additional research and identified insights. We generated a broad problem statement and developed a PoV statement that we then used to guide ideation. We brainstormed, role-played, and storyboarded ideas with each other and with RCWS practitioners at various stages of their careers, and we then went through these ideas and analyzed each for relevance, value, and accessibility in relation to our audience (user) and their need(s). We prototyped (drafted), tested, and gathered feedback from users ranging from colleagues down the hall to editors we've worked with in the past. We used that feedback to generate new iterations both of the prototype and of our problem definition. Many iterations later, many rounds of feedback later, we produced this text.

This production process is likely familiar to students and faculty. Higher education positions us to carry out such a process, one that is deeply connected to the history of rhetoric and, more specifically, to the evolution of the **rhetorical canons** of invention, arrangement, style, memory, and delivery. From the time of the ancient Greek and Roman rhetoricians, each of these canons has undergone renewed calls for their uses and revised visions for how writers can apply them to the contexts from which they are writing. Today is no different. We experience technological and media shifts and evolutions, cultural change, and social differences, and yet we continue to rely on rhetorical thinking; our practices are grounded in these canons. Rhetorical thinking, in turn, informs our problem-solving and the design decisions we make. We can see these five canons when we empathize, define, ideate, prototype, and test.

1.3 Linear and Lateral Thinking

Design thinking requires not only rhetorical reflection of the six stages, but both linear thinking and lateral thinking, too. Often, you will move between both without necessarily recognizing you're in one or the other. The ideation stage expressly necessitates that you engage in lateral thinking, for example, to generate without critique and to seek the novel idea over the relevant solution. However, when you have established the map of possibilities, you will likely return to a more linear thought process to begin determining value and relevance as you prepare for prototyping. And, while iterations require linear thought, you also engage [re]vision laterally.

Arguably, we are likely most familiar with **linear thinking**, which uses a logical, systematic approach to problem-solving, as shown in Figure 1.4. Linear thinking has its place in designing professional documents; as professionals, we are familiar with the central role that audience expectation plays in composing. For many of us, analytically approaching a problem probably calls to mind the philosophers, theorists, and practitioners who built our field's body of knowledge.

Applying linear thinking to document design might lead you to look at models within the genre you are working in and duplicate them within the boundaries you've identified. For example, you might look at a series of assignment prompts, or instructions, in your courses and determine that the genre (assignment prompt) requires that you begin with the purpose of the assignment followed by a description of the desired product and end with an overview of the expectations. This is a well-enough structure to replicate, and it's served many students well, historically.

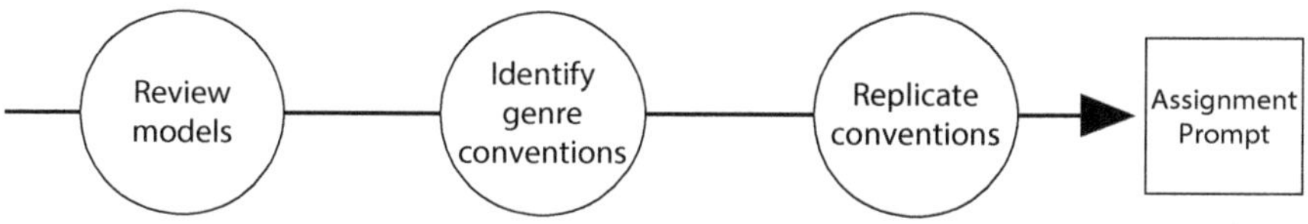

FIGURE 1.4 Linear thinking example.

This image represents the straightforward, often logical, progression of linear thought.

However, many assignment prompt genre conventions are designed to serve neurotypical students and students who have had the privilege of access to technology, educational affordances, and sociocultural advantages (i.e., students who read and process linear, alphabetic texts in ways that are deemed "standard" or "typical"). Many of us have students who do not read and process linear, alphabetic texts well or who struggle with "text walls," or long blocks of text strung together (kind of like what you're currently reading). These students (the neurodivergent students, those without access to "typical" assignment designs, or those who simply learn *differently* than the "standard") might not be served as well by these conventions as neurotypical learners or privileged learners.

We don't believe it was ever sufficient to design solely from a linear perspective; to problem-solve specific documents, audience needs, and achievable outcomes, we must continually weave among linear and lateral thinking patterns. **Lateral thinking** asks you to disrupt your understanding of expectations and constraints in an attempt to identify creative solutions and approaches to problem-solving. Using the same example of designing an assignment prompt for a course, you might brainstorm ways to break up the text visually or ways to present the assignment as the steps students will need to take in order to create the desired product. You might ask your colleagues to help you find alternative ways to present the information, consider using audio or making a video instead of a written assignment prompt, and you might also consider what would happen if you didn't have a prompt at all. Lateral thinking can take us in unexpected directions, lead us to ask unconventional questions and generate novel responses, and potentially facilitate advocacy and equitable design practices.

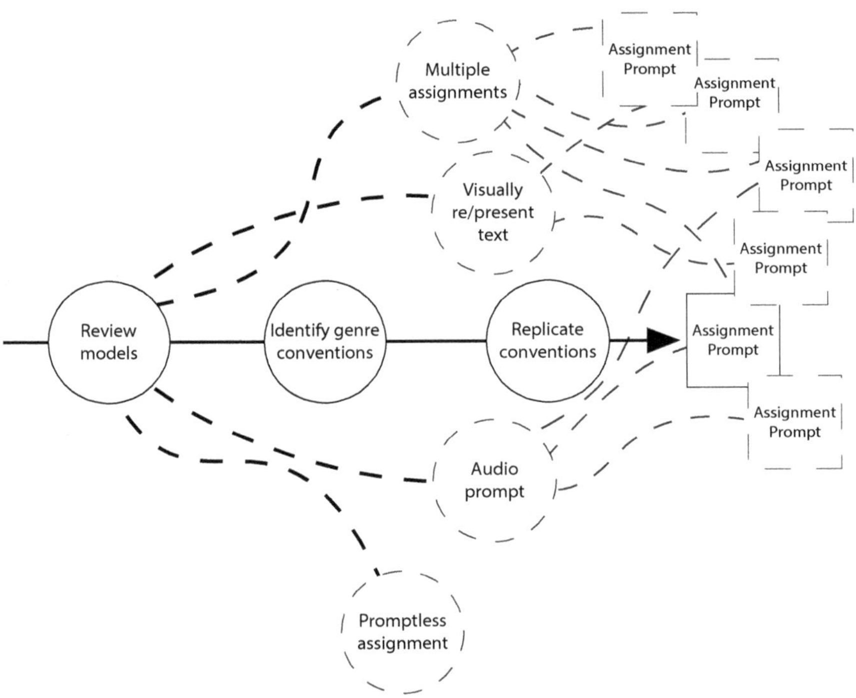

FIGURE 1.5 Linear thinking model with lateral thinking.

This image builds onto the linear thinking model by representing lateral thinking using dashed lines. Here, what we might do when employing linear thinking is represented as the throughline in the center of the image, while the ideas and products connected by dashed lines represent the creative possibilities that we rely on when employing lateral thinking.

In Figure 1.5, the solid line represents the straightforward, logical nature of linear thinking, and the remaining content illustrates the chaotic nature of lateral thinking. While both linear and lateral thinking require you to consider the full context of a problem, the dynamic nature of lateral thinking might facilitate developing a new approach to a possible solution or a new way of thinking about and using information. As illustrated in Figure 1.5, lateral thinking unflattens the processes and products of linear work; it accounts for the complexities of multiple perspectives, user needs and experiences, and contextual differences. Lateral thinking can add dimensionality to your problem-solving and design processes, as well as to your approaches to everyday work and life. As you work through the activities and exercises in this book, you'll be tasked with integrating these frameworks in different ways. Some activities will encourage a more linear approach; some will prioritize lateral thinking. Others will ask you to engage in both linear and lateral thinking to problem-solve a document design.

If you're looking for a starting point for lateral thinking, it may be helpful to return to the categories we frequently use in the empathy stage of design thinking. Here are some questions to consider as you begin generating ideas using lateral thinking:

TABLE 1.4 Problem-Solving Questions Using Lateral Thinking

Think	Feel
• What are some unique possibilities for this situation? • What are new perspectives on this situation? • What (hidden) assumptions or biases exist in the situation? • How might user decision-making processes change if AI could visualize their perception of the situation? • What would change if users had an AI partner to offer different perspectives?	• What (hidden) emotional need(s) does this situation create for users? • How would the situation change if users' emotional responses were visible to others? • How would user response change if the situation occurred in a different professional or cultural context? • How would the situation transform if AI could visualize the emotional climate of the primary user group (i.e., audience)?
Say	**Do**
• How could this situation be explained in only five words? • What metaphors are used to describe this situation? How can these be used to create new solutions? • How would someone from a different discipline, culture, or industry describe this situation? • If AI could detect inconsistencies between what people say they want and what they actually need, how would that transform the problem space?	• What past actions have you or users (i.e., your audience) taken that might influence this situation? • What kinds of actions (or steps) apply to this situation? • What kinds of texts have you created that apply to this situation? • How would user behavior change if AI provided instantaneous feedback on this situation? • What if users engaged the situation with limitations they don't normally have? • What if you reversed the sequence of actions users currently take in this situation? What insights emerge?

(*Continued*)

TABLE 1.4 (Continued)

Alternatively, considering a few "what ifs" may help you get started too:

What if...

- the constraints are removed from the situation?
- the solution failed? What might the implications be?
- you were the user?
- AI could help users adopt alternative thinking styles (e.g., from different professions, disciplines, or cultures)?
- the perceived constraints of the situation were actually strengths?
- the situation was resituated to meet a different need?
- AI could improve how users engage in this situation?

These questions are merely a starting point. It's helpful to take a moment and consider additional questions that are well-suited to the situation you are working to problem-solve and to how you (and your team, if you're working collaboratively) approach ideation.

We might also consider lateral thinking's role in problem-solving a dilemma many practitioners face: how to capture the fluidity of your work in ways that are intelligible across multiple disciplines and beyond the academy. Using the traditional, distinct categories of teaching, research, service, and administration doesn't always effectively capture and communicate all that we do. Thinking laterally, however, may help you to push back against traditional thinking in more dynamic ways by promoting the conceptualization of your work as more than just one thing. For example, when you think about your CV and the experiences it is supposed to represent, you may find that lateral thinking could help you generate better possibilities for representing all that you did in those experiences.

1.4 Scenario: Categorizing Your Work

Imagine you are a second-year assistant professor at an institution that requires high teaching activity and equally values research, service, and administration. Your institution's merit program financially rewards faculty with outstanding performance in all three areas and allows faculty to submit an application annually. The application's instructions require brief statements that illustrate exceptional performance in the categories of *teaching*, *research*, and *service and administration*. In the application, applicants must detail their activities in each category for consideration in a Microsoft Word table. The instructions restrict you from including a lengthy explanation and instead encourage you to use bulleted lists.

During your second year at the institution, you successfully introduced a new local chapter of your discipline's national honor society on your campus, and you coordinated networking events between students and local professionals in the field. These events led you to also develop an internship program, giving students opportunities to work with professionals at field sites. To build this program, you developed a web presence, organized informational meetings, and made arrangements for students to visit the field sites.

In addition, you have taught a total of eight courses this year, which include first-year courses and advanced courses. You also serve on one college committee, a curriculum committee that reviews and approves curriculum proposals.

You want to submit a merit application but are challenged by the overlapping categories your work falls into, and you're concerned that the lack of publications and committee service will not communicate "outstanding performance" in the areas of research and service.

The following activity positions you to explore the dimensionality of academic work through both linear and lateral thinking.

TABLE 1.5 Activity: Unflattening Our Work

Using the scenario, identify which parts represent "teaching," "research," and "service and administration." Then, construct a statement for each category using only the information provided in the scenario. For example, a teaching statement could be "I have taught eight classes this academic year, including ENG 150 Introduction to British Literature, ENG 220 Women and Literature, ENG 270 Environmental Literature, ENG 370 Victorian Literature: Science and Technology, and ENG 410 Seminar: Punk Fiction."

Category	Statement (max. 75 words)
Teaching	
Research	
Service and Administration	

Now, revisit the scenario and consider the *work* of accomplishing each activity noted in it. Then, construct a statement for each category using the dynamic content you've uncovered.

You may want to use the following brief list of questions to help you begin thinking laterally:

- What kinds of activities are required to start a new chapter of a national honor society?
- What kinds of materials are developed in starting a new chapter? Who sees these materials?
- What kinds of activities are involved in serving as an internship coordinator? Teaching first-year and advanced courses? Serving on a curriculum committee?
- What kind of research is needed to start a new chapter of a national honor society? To develop a website? To establish professional connections in your community?

(*Continued*)

TABLE 1.5 (Continued)

Category	Statement (max. 75 words)
Teaching	
Research	
Service and Administration	

Now, consider how your responses change when the categories change. For example, how does separating *service* and *administration* alter how the work is represented? What happens if you create a new category for mentoring? What alternative approaches might you use to represent the work described in this scenario?

1.5 Convergent Design

Just as both linear and lateral thinking play integral roles in design thinking across all its stages, the process also requires divergence and convergence. As Carmen Bueno Muñoz et al. (2024) assert in *Gamification and Design Thinking in Higher Education*, "design thinking models recently developed share certain elements that are essential to implement a design thinking process: (i)teration, convergent-divergent thinking, and flexibility" (location 3.1.3). They note that "Divergent thinking ensures the exploration of various solutions to a problem, while convergent thinking narrows these options to arrive at a final decision" (location 3.1.3). The ideas you generate when you ideate are often referred to as **divergence**. You approach possibility without judgment as you loosen the grip of genre constraints on the ways in which you conceptualize responses to the problem (remember, design thinking is problem-solving).

Between ideation and prototyping, you use analytical thinking to evaluate the value and relevance of the different ideas that you've generated. When you begin to narrow your options through a critical lens, you engage in **convergence**, the very concept this book is about, the concept at the center of our book cover's symbol. This action is crucial to negotiating how far you can push the boundaries of a genre and determining when, where, and how you can break free from constraints and leverage affordances while maintaining a clear understanding of the user experience and design problem. Convergence, then, reiteratively engages both linear and lateral thinking. They are intertwined like our cover's knot represents. You must understand the design context (i.e., genre and audience expectations, content, circulation, etc.) at the same time you must consider how to adapt to address challenges, differences, and opportunities. Recognizing how the moves you make in designing converge together better positions you to be successful in your final products, your documents.

TABLE 1.6 Remix: Categorizing Your Work

Look back to 1.4 Scenario: Categorizing Your Work and consider how you might redesign the way the application captures your work if the design limitations did not exist.

1.5.1 Affordances and Constraints

The final consideration in design development that we want to address here involves parameters. Affordances and constraints each address the limits of a designed object. **Affordances** are simply the actions that an object (whether a technology, a document, a system) allows us to do. When it comes to documents, for instance, affordances are built-in characteristics or features that communicate the documents' possible uses to people. Your contact information on a syllabus affords your students the opportunity to reach you outside of class hours. A search bar on a homepage affords a person the ability to search an entire website.

There are many different types of textual affordances, nonetheless. For example, linguistic affordances could include a designer's use of the first person "I" in their document to afford readers more closeness to the writer or a more subjective viewpoint. Using passive voice instead could afford readers something different: more objectivity or distance between writer and reader or between reader and subject. Affordances can occur not just because of the words in a document but also through the genre or medium the document is written in and on. Digital writing media, like the kind of writing we do for a website, afford users interactivity when they use the text's hyperlinks.

While affordances speak to the possibilities of a text, **constraints** are limitations that are informed by factors in the design and, very possibly, beyond it. Constraints will often include material factors, as well as situational and cultural factors. Certainly, constraints include things like word count and timelines, but they can—and often do—reach far beyond these limitations. For example, returning to our assignment in the previous example (see Section 1.3), we might consider how technology constraints impact student access. If the assignment is only available in an online space, students will have to have internet access to reference the instructions. If students don't have compatible media applications, they may not be able to view the video we included. Depending on the time the student has to complete the assignment and depending on the student's digital literacy skills, they may or may not have the time (or skillset) to identify the application they need to view it.

WHAT AI HAS TO SAY:

Affordances are the built-in features of a document that signal how it can or should be used. They guide readers by making certain actions feel natural or intuitive. Visual elements - like headings, bold text, spacing, and icons - afford scanning, comparison, or emphasis. Digital features such as hyperlinks, search bars, and interactive forms afford navigation, exploration, and input. Even genre conventions can act as affordances: a brochure affords quick browsing, while a policy manual affords careful, sequential reading. In essence, affordances help readers understand the document's purpose and how to interact with it without needing explicit instructions.

This description of affordances assumes that every reader experiences or perceives texts in the same way. It fails to acknowledge, for instance, that readers react differently to document structures depending on variables such as literacy levels or culture.

Constraints are the limits - both internal and external - that shape what a document can be and how it can function. Some constraints are material, such as page size, screen dimensions, printing costs, or accessibility requirements. Others are situational: deadlines, organizational expectations, or the technological environment in which the document will be used. Cultural and rhetorical constraints also play a major role, since different audiences bring different norms, values, and interpretive habits. Constraints aren't just obstacles; they help designers make purposeful choices by narrowing the range of possibilities and ensuring the final document fits its context.

Code credit: Microsoft, *Copilot* (2025, December 12)

The second paragraph doesn't address constraints that result from inequitable systems and lacks discussion of a reader's accessibility needs. For example, design can be constrained by screen-reader compatability or motor-friendly navigation.

Example AI output generated with the prompt: "Explain affordances and constraints in document design in two detailed paragraphs." Code credit: Microsoft, *Copilot* (2025, December 12).

Constraints and affordances are frequently interdependent. Considering what your audience *has* is just as beneficial, if not more so, as considering what your audience *lacks*, and both of these points of reference influence how you determine affordances. As our annotations of the "What AI Has to Say" output demonstrate, affordances and constraints are complex and often include social and cultural considerations. However, the idea that affordances can encourage an intuitive aspect in a design and constraints help designers align with context and use are helpful ways to conceptualize these frameworks. For example, when you consider what technologies your user has access to and how they are likely to use that technology while interacting with your document, you may be more inclined to integrate alternative text for document readers and to use accessible color combinations because you are equitably considering possible interactions that could differ from your own.

Being purposeful in your design thinking process by carefully identifying both affordances and constraints will help you in your quest to mitigate potential bias and prejudices that could impact your audiences (in this case, your students) in negative ways. Likewise, acknowledging possibilities for misunderstandings through divergence enables you then to be better equipped for convergence. You'll want the point of convergence to be the best possible outcome.

TABLE 1.7 Remix: Affordances and Constraints

Constraints can inform affordances. Identify a professional document you've recently developed (e.g., cover letter, research proposal, and assignment) and list the affordances already in your design. Then consider your design constraints (content and user) and identify three elements you could revise or invent to address these constraints.

Document:

Affordances	Constraints	New/Revised Elements

1.6 Adapting to Opportunity

As you move between divergent and convergent design, and as you identify constraints and affordances, you also likely begin to identify ways you can adapt to existing expectations and ways you can challenge them. Here, again, as you consider the divergent design ideas you have generated and question their value and relevance, you may find benefits for your users if your documents eschew specific genre conventions and design choices. You may integrate elements of different ideas in order to better meet the user needs, or you may find affordances that are no longer needed. For example, it behooves you as an academic to find ways to articulate your teaching not only as teaching, but also as research and as service. Lateral approaches and divergent ideas can afford you the possibility of networking your activities across the categories that you are called on to identify your work through in order to be quantified on an assessment level.

In addition to new approaches to content, convergent design may also help you identify inequities and antiquated "norms" in your document designs. Just as you may have retired "references available upon request" from CVs and resumes, you may realize your audience doesn't review hard copies anymore or that you may need to assist readers in finding your content beyond the boundaries of a CV or resume document. As a result, your designs may more commonly integrate hyperlinks, QR codes, embedded files, and so on. Perhaps you will lead readers to publicly shared visual content that your students composed in your classes, or to a website that brings together your most pertinent and valuable work. Some of these design choices are already in motion; many academics are already participating in forward design and creating supplemental materials to standard genre documents.

1.7 Scenario: Developing Assignments

You've been hired at an urban university as an adjunct instructor to teach an introductory course in your discipline. The hiring department has asked you to design the first major assignment for the course, and you are required to integrate supplemental materials and activities to support this assignment (i.e., readings, technology demonstrations, workshops, etc.). The assignment should take students two weeks to complete and will count for 10% of the final grade for the course.

In Table 1.8, you will approach the assignment design through lateral thinking, prioritizing the potential technological and experiential inequities of the students and the affordances of the university.

TABLE 1.8 Activity: Dynamically Designing Assignments

Design an assignment for Section 1.7's scenario and gather/create the supporting materials and activities. Consider the affordances and privileges pertaining to you, your students, and the university, and how you can potentially challenge the existing genre expectations of an assignment and/or its prompt in meaningful ways to meet the contextual needs of the students and the course.

Now that you have designed an assignment, take a moment to reflect on this experience, making note of what worked and what did not in your approach. Reflection is one way we review our work; it is a way of thinking through our actions and choices that enables us to grow as designers. To "see" what we have created, we might ask: What came easily? What was a challenge? What could happen differently next time? Answering these questions allows us time to think about how we design in the first place. That is, it helps us to see the multitude of paths we take to solve a design problem.

TABLE 1.9 Remix: AI and Assignment Development

Using the activity in Table 1.8, consider how you could leverage AI in your assignment (and/or supplemental materials and activities) to facilitate students deepening their understanding of AI and the ethics of AI applications. How could you integrate AI into your students' process to complete the assignment (or activities)? How would this reshape your assignment design?

As we conclude this chapter, we encourage you to look for opportunities throughout the design process to make changes—big and small—and to consider the potential impact these changes may have not only on the document's genre, but on the audience and the content, too. RCWS faculty have consistently adapted to changing circumstances by relying on rhetorical thinking to seek out *possibilities*, and we hope you will too. Adding convergent design practices to your repertoire can drive equitable communication and education practices forward. As you read this book, think about how the examples illustrate equity and inclusion and how the activities challenge you to design with a contemporary audience in mind. For instance, the CV example in Section 1.2 Understanding Design Thinking calls for redesigning "Teaching Experience" to "Pedagogical Experience" to spotlight competencies instead of courses taught. Here, the competencies speak to skills learned rather than to time in a classroom. Reflecting on the rhetorical nature of your work, you will be better able to call for change on your campus, in your field, and across disciplines. You are well-suited to show others why and how adapting to opportunities can lead to more equitable practices for faculty and students alike.

1.8 Chapter 1 Review

In this chapter, we introduced key terms, concepts, and strategies for problem-solving the creation and circulation of your documents. Before moving on to the next chapter, take a moment to reflect on:

- the role of empathizing, defining, ideating, prototyping, testing, iterating, as well as thinking linearly and laterally, in design thinking;
- design thinking as a way for academics to approach documents as opportunities to address their concerns by centering the writer and user, rather than the genre expectations;
- leveraging divergence and convergence to rethink genre conventions and create forward-thinking documents that effectively meet both writer and reader needs;
- the importance of identifying when and how to effectively challenge expectations and boundaries in convergent design.

References

Bueno Muñoz, Carmen, Hernández Nanclares, Núria, Murillo Zamorano, Luis R., & López Sánchez, José Ángel. (2024). *Gamification and design thinking in higher education: Case studies for instructional innovation in the Economics classroom*. Routledge.

d.school. (n.d.). *An introduction to design thinking: Process guide*. Hasso Plattner Institute of Design at Stanford. Retrieved on January 12, 2026, from https://web.stanford.edu/~mshanks/MichaelShanks/files/509554.pdf

Gruwell, Leigh. (2022). *Making matters: Craft, ethics, and new materialist rhetorics*. University Press of Colorado.

Johnson-Eilola, Johndan, & Selber, Stuart. (2007). Plagiarism, originality, and assemblage. *Computers and Composition*, *24*(4), 375–403.

Kress, Gunther. (2010). *Multimodality: A social semiotic approach to contemporary communication*. Routledge.

Marback, Richard. (2009). Embracing wicked problems: The turn to design in Composition Studies. *College Composition and Communication*, *61*(2), W397–W419.

Microsoft. (2025, December 12). *Copilot* [Large Language Model]. https://copilot.microsoft.com

Palmeri, Jason. (2012). *Remixing composition: A history of multimodal writing pedagogy*. NCTE.

Purdy, James P. (2014). What can design thinking offer Writing Studies? *College Composition and Communication*, *65*(4), 612–641. https://www.jstor.org/stable/43490875

Shipka, Jody. (2011). *Toward a composition made whole*. University of Pittsburgh Press.

Sirc, Geoffrey. (2002). *English composition as a happening*. University Press of Colorado.

Tham, Jason C. K. (Ed.). (2022). *Keywords in design thinking: A lexical primer for technical communicators & designers*. WAC Clearinghouse; University Press of Colorado. https://wac.colostate.edu/books/tpc/design/

Wible, Scott. (2020). Using design thinking to teach creative problem solving in writing courses. *College Composition and Communication*, *71*(3), 399–425.

Yancey, Kathleen Blake, & McElroy, Stephen. (Eds.). (2017). *Assembling composition*. NCTE.

2

AI, WRITING, AND DESIGN

2.1 Working with Artificial Intelligence

Over the last five years, the evolution of artificial intelligence (AI) and specifically generative AI (GenAI) and large language models (LLMs) have brought about new opportunities and challenges for designers of documents. As you navigate your current academic experience, you may be coming to this text with your own experiences using AI tools. Universities and colleges around the globe have had mixed responses to AI tools, particularly GenAI. Some have welcomed the tools, encouraging their use and helping to develop them. Some have warned of their pitfalls and spotlighted their shortcomings, restricting or banning faculty and student use. What this tells us is that school administrators, faculty, and students seem to have differing understandings of AI and when and how to use it.

When it comes to writing, proponents of AI tout generative AI as revolutionary, suggesting that it will change the way we write with never-before-seen opportunities in addition to improving our writing efficiency and accuracy. Time will tell if this proves true or not, but one thing is for certain: AI was and continues to be built upon two technologies, language and writing.

AI is often used as an umbrella term, encompassing any hardware or software that takes on tasks that humans normally do, like learning and analysis. A self-driving car, most search engines, "smart" features in household appliances, navigation apps, and the facial recognition feature in your phone are just a few examples of AI we find in our daily lives (or may in the near future). AI improves, predicts, and makes decisions by learning patterns from data input by its owners and users. These data include language and writing.

DOI: 10.4324/9781003717232-4

LLMs are a type of AI that are trained on large amounts of human language so that they can in turn generate human-like language outputs for their users. ChatGPT, Copilot, Claude, and Perplexity are just a few current examples of popular LLMs. When you prompt ChatGPT, you do so through language and writing. ChatGPT then formulates a response based on its training on other large amounts of language and writing. All LLMs are AI, but not all AI are LLMs. Although you use language when you prompt Spotify to give you music recommendations, its AI isn't based on a language model, but rather on your algorithm, your past history/activity using Spotify.

GenAI refers to the group of AI that generate content. So, GenAI includes LLMs, as well as image generators that produce static and dynamic visual output, and sonic generators that produce music and audio output, rendering generators that produce 3D models, and coding generators that produce, translate, and debug code. GenAI is a special kind of AI as it not only analyzes data, but it then goes on to create or design things, like documents, videos, audio samples, virtual environments, and so forth.

As we noted in the introduction, GenAI demands human work and self-awareness. In other words, we must be aware that we are using a tool that is not human, but that is created by humans to produce human-like answers. AI is reliant on you, the writer, to critically and successfully leverage its output. To date, best practices suggest that AI output needs human vetting, contextualizing, and revising to best meet audience needs. In other words, AI requires active, rather than passive, human *work*.

AI doesn't "think" or "reflect" like humans do; rather, it analyzes patterns in a set of data to produce the most probable output for the prompt you give it based on the data it is trained on. Therefore, it is never 100% accurate or representative of everyone and every culture. Ask Copilot to write a paragraph about how fast a cheetah can run and the output is apt to be factually accurate, even if the paragraph likely needs stylistic revision. But, more complex tasks, like asking it to explain the process for developing an ethically-grounded conflict resolution dialog for global sites of unrest, will likely generate inaccurate output that may include missing citations, inaccurate quotes in a literature review, or mislabeled charts and skewed evidence. Output may appear to be close to the truth or sound somewhat correct—humans who are less familiar with conflict resolution research and scholarship may not even notice. But, those who are aware will likely find the output in need of that human work: making sure the missing citations are found, accurately quoting, clarifying vague content, and so forth. These inaccuracies, whether vaguely misleading or entirely fabricated, are what we call "hallucinations," output that may be plausible but not precise or completely truthful.

Even still, some would argue that it doesn't matter if the output isn't completely accurate or well organized; it is close enough. They might argue that time is limited and we must consider the time revision and correction take; if it is close enough, who cares?

You should care. As ethical academics and writers, we all should care. Misinformation and misrepresentation can have devastating consequences. Using GenAI ethically *requires* human work. Even using GenAI to generate something as simple as an email demands human work: we must review its content for accuracy, revise it to sound like our voice, fine-tune the organization and word choice, and so on. Efficiency and accuracy rely on **humans in the loop (HITL)**. With that being said, we need to remind you that HITL is a part of a human work strategy, but they are not synonymous.

Furthermore, **AI output**, the materials you receive from a GenAI you've prompted, may not take into consideration issues of class, race, or gender when compiling its response. Likely, the AI has been trained on the dominant discourses of those in power, not on minority voices. In addition to checking for accuracy, we need to also be cognizant of the voices that AI excludes and the biased outputs that it can create so that we may not perpetuate these.

When done ethically, working with GenAI doesn't enhance or devalue what you're already doing; it's just incorporating a different tool. Like with any learning you have done, integrating it into your writing and design process will likely be slow at first—getting to know the steps you must take, the limitations of the technology, the critical analysis it requires, etc.—but eventually this work will balance out with the rest of the work you do. The first time you learn to grade an essay, for example, you might find it difficult; it may take you a lot of time to get through reading it and making meaningful comments to your student. But, eventually, you get better at it; one day, you will be as effective and efficient in your grading as senior faculty.

The human work you need to do when designing documents starts by weighing the AI tools you are using with 1) how you use them and 2) why you use them. In other words, you must use a rhetorical approach, one that examines (you) the writer, your audience, your purpose, your intended text, and your context. This work will take time as you will have to learn and adapt while using and training your AI tools. The human work you will do will likely require research and reflection in which you situate yourself and others in the process. Writing doesn't happen in a bubble after all. This process of writing with AI tools to produce your documents will require rhetorical reflection time and again as you understand, design, research, and revise. Put simply, to successfully design a document with AI, your process might look something like the following image. This process will likely be a recursive one rather than a linear one, though both linear and lateral thinking will be involved.

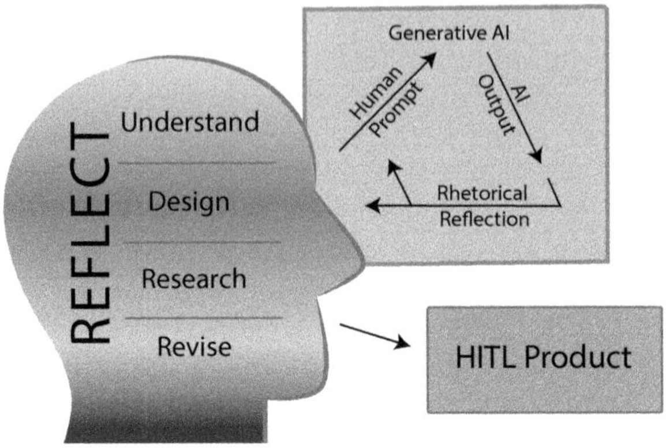

Illustration of recursive workflow when composing with AI.

Critical, ethical AI collaboration isn't just about being critical about the outputs; we should also be critical of our inputs too. Asking "What role did I play in this output?" is also important because we play a significant role in what the AI produces. From the prompts we input to the data we share, we're contributing to how companies build AI in the ways they do. We give them our permission, both directly and indirectly, to build and train AI; importantly, outputs are shaped by these actions. We must think rhetorically about our use of AI, as well as the information we provide it.

2.1.1 Understand

AI tools offer promising opportunities but not all designing tasks should include the use of them. Indeed, using AI tools must begin with rhetorical reflection; this will help you understand the point of your writing task. After all, you must have a good grasp of what you are trying to design and what you wish to accomplish with your document. This reflection can also serve your understanding of the AI tool itself, why you are choosing it over others, and what it can and cannot do. Understanding your answers to these questions provides a good foundation for moving forward with the design of your document. This act of reflecting in order to understand is best summarized in the following worksheet. Work your way through the questions, making note of your answers. These will help you understand whether to proceed with the help of an AI tool and then help you build the prompt you will input into the AI tool.

TABLE 2.1 Rhetorical Reflection Worksheet for Understanding

Rhetorical Element	*Questions to Answer*
Writer/designer of the document	Why am I writing the document? What do I get from writing the document? What do I know about the AI tool? What does the AI tool do? What does the AI tool not do?
Purpose for your document	What is the goal for my document? How will the AI tool help me accomplish this goal?
Audience for your document	Who is my audience for the document? How can I use the AI tool to learn more about my audience? How can I teach the AI tool about my audience?
Text of document and subject matter/content of the document	What does the AI tool know about the type of document I am writing? What subject matter will I need the AI tool to help me learn more about? What content can the AI tool help me create?
Context for which you are writing the document	How can I use the AI tool to learn more about my context for writing? What does the AI tool know about the context for my writing?

Answering these questions will not always be easy. For example, how can we know what the AI tool's understanding of a genre is and how it came to that understanding beyond what we tell it? As we will discuss later, it may not be possible to know everything about an AI tool. For instance, sometimes a company that owns and develops a tool may not offer the public a transparent explanation as to how they created it and how they continue to shape and develop it over time. When this is the case, we have to rely on our own experiences and observations, as well as those of others who use the tool, to best understand our rhetorical situation.

TABLE 2.2 Activity: White Paper

Your dean has launched a new interdisciplinary certificate program for students and has asked your department to create a new interdisciplinary course for it, one that combines one of your department's disciplines with another discipline in your college. It will be a three-credit course that meets twice a week for 75 minutes and will be co-taught by two instructors. Since you are unsure how your discipline could relate to another discipline, you decide to use a GenAI tool, like Copilot or ChatGPT, to help you create a white paper for your department that explains and demonstrates connections between disciplinary pedagogies. Before you can prompt GenAI, work your way through the rhetorical worksheet in Table 2.1 to understand how and why you will use AI to create the white paper. Write down your answers to the questions and keep them for the other activities in this chapter.

Reflection on AI should also include an honest attempt at recognizing common myths about it, including those you believe, and then dispelling them. We can identify these myths by considering current ideas and conversations on GenAI. For example, one of the most common things we hear as educators from our students is that using AI saves them time. Take a moment to explore the myth "GenAI saves time." Consider how you might begin this investigation. Perhaps, you start by asking critical questions like: What does saving time really mean? Does it mean a reduction in labor for humans? What would the labor humans perform to complete a task with and without GenAI even be? And how would we define this labor? In answering such questions, you are reflecting on what is gained and what is lost, and what value we place on these gains and losses. Important to this grand myth surrounding GenAI's use, we must assess if speed is really a good thing in the context in which we are working. Is it possible that in saving time we lose quality?

Identifying and understanding the ideas driving us to work with GenAI and influencing the ways in which we do that work or represent it can help develop a critical awareness of your engagement with the tool. Additionally, your answers to critical questions like the ones posed here will likely lead you to additional ways in which to dispel the myth (and other myths like it) for yourself and for others. You likely might find yourself researching and verifying evidence, speaking to experts about technology, assessing the statement for bias, understanding how and where the myth originated and why, and so on. When we dispel myths on AI, what we are really doing is giving ourselves a moment to bring choice to the foreground, realign with values important to inclusive design, and prevent ourselves from making automatic design decisions with AI that could ultimately perpetuate those myths.

2.1.2 Design

Once you begin to understand your task and the AI tool you will use, you will start to design your prompt or input for the AI tool. This prompt will direct the AI tool to generate something for you—in other words, an output. In designing the prompt, you will need to include your parameters or instructions for the AI to follow in generating the output. Choose your words carefully based on the information you gathered when reflecting on your understanding of your task and tool. This means engineering phrases and sentences that best capture what you want the tool to accomplish in its output. This may involve choosing specific words with the goal of being as clear as possible.

Designing a prompt for AI is recursive, meaning it will likely require you to start with an initial prompt (or several) and revise that after you get your first generated output. You'll learn more about revising later in this chapter.

For now, we suggest that you reflect again, this time focusing on your prompt and answering questions that will help you design it. Table 2.3 can help with this:

TABLE 2.3 Rhetorical Reflection Worksheet for Designing

Writer/designer	What does the AI tool need to know about me? Will the words I use in my prompt generate what I need?
Purpose	What does the AI tool need to know about my purpose for writing?
Audience	What do I need to tell the AI tool about my audience? What will my audience expect and/or tolerate from AI?
Text	What information does AI need to know about the type of document I am writing? What language should I use to create my prompt? What tone should I use? What word choices should I make? What are other ways of saying this prompt?
Context	What information does AI need to know about the context in which I am writing?

Syntax, or sentence structure, plays a prominent role in crafting prompts for GenAI. Having an awareness of the relationships between words in a sentence and in what order they appear (subject, verb, object, etc.) spotlights how these relationships create meaning. Likewise, we can often write a sentence in different ways, still maintaining the central meaning. In other words, you can use iterations, a term you learned about in Chapter 1. Remember that AI looks for patterns based on the prompt you enter. Using different syntax in your prompts may generate different outputs because the tool will look for patterns in different ways. Also, it is important to note that different languages have different syntactic rules. In English, we typically use the subject-verb-object order. But, that is not the case in other languages. You might consider what languages your tool has been trained on to determine what choices you will make with your prompts.

TABLE 2.4 Activity: Writing Prompts for AI

Using your answers from the activity in Table 2.2 for creating a white paper, create a list of initial prompts for a GenAI tool. Think of this as prototyping. The prompts should help you generate outputs to write a white paper. As a reminder, you are trying to create a white paper for your department that explains and demonstrates connections between disciplinary pedagogies. Create several prompts that you can test out in a later activity in this chapter.

2.1.3 Research

Building your prompts and analyzing the output from a GenAI tool will often include research. Research helps ensure you are asking the right questions or writing good instructions for the tool as well as verifies whether or not the output are accurate and true. Throughout this chapter, you have learned that researching the tool you plan to use is important. But, learning more about your prompt is just as important. In previous activities, you were encouraged to reflect on your rhetorical situation. This reflection asked you to think about your context for writing. In this case, you are writing about your college and how you can develop an interdisciplinary course. You may not be familiar with every discipline and instructor in your college, especially those outside your department. You may need to spend time gathering information from your college as a result. GenAI could help you do this research, but it should not be the only place you conduct your research. Speaking with faculty, for instance, would be a good way to find out more about what other instructors are teaching and how they feel about collaborating on an interdisciplinary course.

If you recall from a previous chapter, empathizing can help you construct effective documents because it helps you envision the perspectives of your audience. GenAI cannot always empathize with your audience; therefore, you may need to conduct research to find out more about your audience in order to connect with them. This research might include finding out what your audience values, what might be a source of reservation, and/or what might inspire them. You can then address these issues in a number of ways in your writing. For instance, researching using empathy can help you determine what tone of voice, jargon, and metaphors to use with your audience.

Prompt writing is a recursive process and once you begin to use this in your research and writing processes, you will need to analyze and research your output. After all, how can you confirm the accuracy of an output without research? To assist you with the examination of your output, Table 2.5 can get you started with a rhetorical approach.

TABLE 2.5 Rhetorical Reflection Worksheet for Researching AI Output

Writer/designer	What are my initial thoughts on the outputs? What do I know about the output? What are my capabilities for researching these outputs further?
Purpose	How will the outputs help me achieve my purpose?
Audience	Will my audience understand these outputs? Would these outputs be expected?
Text	How accurate are the outputs? What needs to be researched further?
Context	Do the outputs match the context in which I am writing?

As mentioned in the beginning of this chapter, output often contain hallucinations that require human work to flesh them out and revise them. Think of this process as testing, a concept introduced in the previous chapter. As you analyze the output, you'll likely find that follow-up prompts or revised prompts are necessary if you want to continue engaging GenAI as part of your process. However, the extent to which you're using GenAI will differ with each project and each rhetorical situation.

TABLE 2.6 Activity: Researching Output

After inputting your prompts from Table 2.4: Activity: Writing Prompts for AI, go through the outputs thoroughly using the worksheet in Table 2.5: Rhetorical Reflection Worksheet for Researching AI Output. Spend time researching them carefully to ensure they are accurate and that they also meet the demands of the situation.

The output might spark additional ideas that need to be researched as well. Using GenAI to create pathways to meander through as you develop your work can be beneficial, especially if you are trying to generate an abundance of ideas. This is what recursive writing and research look like.

2.1.4 Revise

To use a GenAI tool purposefully and effectively, you're likely going to develop and revise your prompts several times, considering the output and your goal(s) each time. As you review and vet the output, you will find useful content that you can then revise for tone and voice.

TABLE 2.7 Rhetorical Reflection Worksheet for Revising AI Output

Writer/designer	Do the outputs sound like me? Do they need to? Does the output reflect my values?
Purpose	How does the output reflect my purpose? Are the tone and content appropriate to my purpose?
Audience	Do the outputs help me meet my ethical obligations to my audience? Does the output include assumptions or biased representations of my audience?
Text	Do the outputs sound humanlike? Natural? Generic? Are there gaps or missing information in the output? Can I trust the information in the output?
Context	Does the output meet expectations for this genre or professional situation? How does the output connect to existing conversations that share this context? How do I need to attribute the output that I use?

Think of revising your AI prompt as critical thinking. In exploring the different ways we might approach GenAI, J.J. Sylvia IV and Carol Reeves (2024) posit "that prompting *is* thinking, the back-and-forth process of responding to a GAI output with better prompts *is* critical thinking, even a form of dialogue" (p. 363). That back-and-forth process is what you will find here in this book and in this chapter specifically. Humans have been using such a process since they began to think and use tools. It is a process we should not fear. As Sylvia and Reeves go on to say, "We might accept, and even embrace, the inevitable capacity of technology to change our brains, to alter and refine our thinking" (p. 363). In other words, we should not view AI as replacing our ability to think for ourselves, but rather find ways in which AI can help our thinking. This approach reinforces HITL practices. This is not the first time a new technology has changed how and why humans write, and it won't be the last. For a brief history of this, see Sylvia and Reeves. Humans have proven over time that they can adapt and find ways to still be a human in the writing process despite using new technologies.

TABLE 2.8 Activity: Revising Prompts and Output

You've practiced many of the steps included in the outline below in this chapter's previous activities. Refer to the prompts you crafted for Table 2.4: Writing Prompts for AI and complete the following. It may be helpful to refer to all four of the rhetorical reflection worksheets in this chapter as you move through each step of the following workflow:
Prompt 1:
Output 1:
My Observations:
Prompt 2: (Revision of prompt 1)
Output 2:
My Observations:
Compare and Contrast: (Describe the differences between output 1 and output 2)
What I Need Research:
What I Need to Revise:

Putting together the four processes of understanding, designing, researching, and revising for GenAI use, you may work with a basic workflow like the one provided in Table 2.8.

2.2 AI and Lateral Thinking

Using GenAI and lateral thinking means finding all the available means and possibilities for your writing. Lateral thinking is about the unexpected, the unique options for your writing situation. The irony of this is that the

AI cannot think on its own; it just looks for patterns on what already exists. So how, then, can we use it to imagine possibilities? And do we want it to help us do this imagining? Do we want to forgo the mental exercise of pushing ourselves to be creative?

These are the questions that educators and scholars are currently contemplating as AI evolves and schools adapt to its uses. In "Large Language Models Write Answers," Annette Vee (2023) argues, for example, that we cannot let LLMs take away students' ability to participate in critical inquiry and "writing for productive uncertainty" (p. 178). She makes a case that LLMs have created a "model of writing for right answers" (p. 178) leaving little room for students to think creatively and to ponder deeply complex issues.

Perhaps, this isn't an either/or argument. Perhaps, a better way to think of using AI is to think of it as a tester for your lateral thinking. Lateral thinking requires creative engagement, and AI cannot necessarily do that. But it can test your ideas in a low-stakes environment that might lead you to new ways of thinking. A GenAI space can be a collaborative playground, albeit a limited one. You can put in an idea and ask it to provide feedback, give you scenarios, respond in a specific persona, all of which could aid you in finding additional possibilities for your writing. For instance, using AI to help you with your lateral thinking could be a more accessible route than trying to find an audience to test different iterations of your ideas. It can simulate a sample of your audience, a focus group, and/or a pilot study.

Using the information gathered from the activities earlier in this chapter, you could use AI to think about all the possibilities for writing a white paper for your department. You could identify components of a white paper and then ask a GenAI tool to provide you with three different templates for a white paper based on those components and three that deviate from those components. Examining those templates could help you see what you are missing and lead you to think in new ways.

To take this playground concept a step further, you could set up your AI tool to be a collaborator. Essentially, an **AI collaborator** acts like an agent that meaningfully contributes to your work, whether that's writing, research, or design. Many GenAI tools allow users to set up parameters, which are saved settings that define the AI's role by providing boundaries. These parameters are different from what you put in your prompt and are often inserted into the settings function of AI tools, which can allow you to connect the collaborator to other tools you use, such as writing applications. The parameters (sometimes called personas) determine the boundaries in which the tool should operate, what decisions it can make, what style it should take on, what perspective it should use, and what history it should account for. Over time, you can use this collaborator again and again, training it as you interact with it and give it feedback.

Interacting with multiple AI collaborators could prove helpful when trying to imagine different possibilities for your writing. Essentially, you can have conversations with different perspectives. Using the white paper example and activities from earlier in this chapter, you could set up several collaborators, each designed to provide a different set of perspectives, and then use them to get a range of responses on your ideas for the white paper.

WHAT AI HAS TO SAY:

To train an AI collaborator that helps improve your writing while including gendered and minority voices without resorting to stereotypes, begin by setting explicit expectations for inclusivity and authenticity in your prompts. Ask the AI to provide diverse perspectives and specify that these should be represented with nuance and respect, avoiding tokenism or oversimplification. Include contextual details—such as cultural, historical, or professional norms—to guide accurate representation. After generating output, critically review it for bias, stereotypes, or language that diminishes agency, and provide corrective feedback to refine future responses. Encourage the AI to draw on credible sources from minority scholars and organizations to ensure depth and accuracy. Finally, make reflection and iteration part of your process, revising prompts and outputs until they align with your voice, purpose, and ethical standards for representation.

Code credit: Microsoft, *Copilot* (2025, December 15)

> Scrutinize your tool's understanding of gendered and minority voices because AI tools are not trained on data that represents everyone. Be aware that AI tools often start from a place of bias and lack a wider, more complex perspective of diversity.

Example AI output generated with the prompt: "Write a detailed paragraph explaining how to train an AI collaborator to improve writing while incorporating gendered and minority voices in nuanced, non-stereotypical ways. Include guidance on setting expectations, prompting for diverse perspectives, reviewing for bias, and iterating." Code credit: Microsoft, *Copilot* (2025, December 15).

Working with an AI collaborator isn't easy as it requires you to actively reflect on the output it generates and to critically think about the assumptions and values these outputs are built upon. As noted in the annotation to Copilot's output, AI technologies may start from a place of bias and from limited representations of diversity. It is up to us, then, to do the human work of guiding its use. That is, we must actively define the ethical parameters for the AI collaborator to work within, and these parameters need to account for diverse voices without misrepresenting them. You may, for instance, need to define what gendered language looks like and how that language can lead to exclusionary knowledge building. Question the outputs and do so often. Indeed, make this sustained effort as you continue to work with your AI collaborator.

2.3 Scenario: Designing an AI Collaborator

For the upcoming year, you plan to write a journal article, a conference presentation, and a grant proposal. These will build on your previous research studies and scholarship and will likely help you make the case for a promotion at the end of the year. To manage this work effectively and efficiently and to ensure consistency across the three projects, you turn to AI. For the first step of this plan, you wish to create literature reviews for each project.

TABLE 2.9 Activity: Designing an AI Collaborator

Using the scenario in Section 2.3, create an AI collaborator that can help you write the literature reviews for all three projects (journal article, conference presentation, and grant proposal). To begin with, find the settings function in a GenAI tool that allows you to save parameters. In these parameters, do the following:

- Define a role for your collaborator (i.e., a research assistant, theorist, archivist, synthesizer). In defining the role, use concrete language to describe characteristics.
- Share some of your previous research and scholarship with the tool so that it becomes familiar with you and your work.
- Develop workflows that instruct the tool how it should complete the work (in this case, a literature review). For example, you could instruct it to summarize specific journal articles published in a particular timeframe using 3-4 paragraphs focused on certain aspects of the scholarship (main arguments, findings, and so forth).

Next, test your collaborator and reflect on its outputs, providing feedback as you use it again. Here are some questions to consider as you do this:

- How do the outputs reflect the parameters you set?
- How do the outputs extend beyond the parameters you set?
- How do the outputs reflect the intentions you had when setting the parameters?
- How do the outputs align with your audience's expectations?
- Do the outputs exclude a population?

Finally, you can engage in activities that probe your GenAI tool for biases, harmful output, and misinformation and do lateral reading with trusted sources.

In the scenario and activity, you considered using an AI collaborator to help you manage the research task of writing literature reviews. After you worked with your collaborator for a while, you were instructed in the activity to probe for bias, harmful output, and misinformation. If you found any, and our guess is that you did, your next step should be to rhetorically reflect on what caused them and how you can react to them in careful and ethically responsible ways. Using AI is far from a smooth process, but it does give us an opportunity for critical reflection that can often lead to better insights and judgment on our part. In other words, breakdowns can lead to learning and growing. Working through the AI's literature reviews, for instance, you might find that the AI output is mischaracterizing a theory. Yet, in reflecting upon this mischaracterization, you think of something you had never thought about before, which then leads you to revise the framework for your journal article into something much more poignant and groundbreaking. As we will discuss later in this book, revising plays a crucial role in the design process. In fact, we would argue that designing is revising. In the case of the literature reviews, the AI collaborator's inability to meet your expectations provided you important (and sometimes unexpected) ways for strengthening your work. Using AI is not the equivalent of a shortcut but rather it is a design choice that can only be successful if you pair it with reflection and revision.

2.4 Affordances, Constraints, and Pushing Back

With these new opportunities and possibilities, you will find that your strategies for writing will adapt. This chapter has already addressed many of the affordances GenAI offers you. It can provide feedback from a range of perspectives and help you generate ideas. It can assist you in organizing your thoughts and learning about unfamiliar genres. It can expedite your writing process and offer concise summaries.

But, just as AI affords us opportunities, there are a multitude of constraints in working with GenAI, too. If you're using AI with source materials, you may find that the output contains false information or counterfeit sources. These hallucinations, if not addressed in your rhetorical revision, can deeply impact your reputation with your readers. Similarly, GenAI has little ability to navigate cultural context, so its output may be mired in stereotypes and biases. Prompting AI to provide its reasoning, link to source materials, and use equitable language and phrasing can reduce some of these issues, but your human oversight and judgment—your work—is the most reliable tool in ensuring accurate and fair content.

Additional constraints to consider include disciplinary limits and technology overhead. Many GenAIs are limited in the kind of information they can access, impacting the quality and value of their output depending on your industry or profession and on your purpose. Some AIs are designed for specific tasks. For example, HealthScribe and UpToDate Expert are used by medical professionals to assist in generating patient notes and diagnosing. These AIs aren't designed to brainstorm structure options for a white paper. Similarly, you wouldn't prompt QuickBooks AI to write a letter; you'd use it for financial insight and management. Ensuring you are using the appropriate AI for your task can help you leverage its affordances.

Technology overhead with GenAI may be one of the more commonly addressed constraints. Primarily, this includes access and cost. The diversity of GenAI isn't limited to its coding; many GenAI platforms have subscription tiers that restrain the AI's ability. A person working with a paid subscription may have the advantage of more accurate content, greater access to personas, and the ability to retain a conversation history. Many AI companies also use a token-based model, which limits the amount of content you can generate during a specific timeframe.

But access and cost are not limited to the user. Although it reaches beyond the scope of this text, these issues also call our attention to the environmental impact of GenAI and the importance of purposeful use. According to the United Nations Environment Programme (UNEP) (2024), the primary environmental concerns include the stress data centers put on existing energy structures, the waste these centers produce, and the water they consume. Importantly, UNEP notes that an AI-assisted Google search consumes ten times the energy than that of its counterpart, a standard Google search. Mindful, purposeful use can minimize the environmental impact of your GenAI interactions.

As you may have already realized, designing responsibly means considering who benefits (and who does not) and in what ways. When considering this in the context of adopting AI technology, such a consideration may mean thinking beyond the materials of the technology itself and considering the companies that build them. In other words, affordances and constraints (and thus the impacts these have) don't always have to be material, technical, or isolated. In addition to the environmental, intellectual, economic, and social impacts, we should also recognize its impact on labor and power relations. Who, for instance, builds, owns, and grants access to AI technologies? Do the companies that build them use ethical labor practices? What pressures do these companies put on local communities where resources are mined? What this shows us is that responsible design, especially if that design includes using AI, is relational, that it is situated and connected in the ecosystems in which it is embedded.

2.5 Adapting to Opportunity

We have to actively seek out opportunities with AI, meaning we have to be in the driver's seat.

For instance, thinking of GenAI as a collaborator in your design process gives you access to opportunities that can help you develop a deeper sense of your strengths and weaknesses as a writer. GenAI can serve as a test-audience for your job documents and/or serve as a "scene partner" to help prepare you for interviews, conference talks, employment negotiations, etc. It can assist in stabilizing your brand content across your documents (i.e., making sure your content uses language and tone consistently in all documents). This is useful for personal professional documents and also for program, department, college, and university-wide documents.

While GenAI can take on your more repetitive tasks, like, for example, asking it to adjust your template of your job cover letter for specific hiring institutions, it presents new development possibilities too. If you don't know code, it can help you develop advanced assets for a web portfolio. If you need help with planning your courses, what lecture or activity you will facilitate in your classrooms, and/or what assignments you will administer, GenAI could provide you with possible choices as well as walk you through how to implement them in your particular context.

2.6 Scenario: Creating an AI-Infused Workflow

Your department chair has asked you to integrate AI activities into two of your courses to meet a new college-wide technology initiative. As an output, you contemplate when and how to use AI, where to locate the human in the process/workflow, and how to get students to engage it critically. In the end, you need to create new syllabi to reflect the AI integrations.

TABLE 2.10 Activity: Creating an AI-Infused Workflow

Using the scenario in Section 2.6, create an AI-infused workflow to help integrate AI into your courses and write your new syllabi. Your workflow should take into consideration the best pedagogical practices in your field in addition to the subject matter of your courses. This workflow should be repeatable for each of your courses. For example, it could look something like this:
Step 1: Synthesize scholarship on the best teaching practices of [subject matter x]. Step 2: Learn current course structure and learning outcomes. Step 3: Propose possible integrations. Step 4: Test integrations and revise based on feedback. Step 5: Incorporate integrations into a syllabus. Step 6: Edit and proofread the syllabus document.

2.7 Ethical Considerations

Many of the companies that build and own AI tools keep their development and training of their tools top secret. We don't necessarily know how an AI tool is developed or with what and whose data. Therefore, what it produces could essentially come from someone else, which can raise questions about plagiarism. There is no easy answer to the question, "What is plagiarism in the age of AI?" If, for instance, you use AI to create an internal grant proposal at your institution, is it really your grant proposal or a combination of other people's work? Traditional definitions of plagiarism often state that plagiarism occurs when a person uses someone's words, ideas, and/or work without giving credit to the original creators. Because

AI is trained on the words, ideas, and work of others and often times does not cite everything in its outputs, humans are left to discern whether using those outputs violates any creator's rights. As of now, it is important to always let your readers know that you have used an AI tool to build your texts. As you have seen in this text, we, the authors, have indicated when we relied on AI in each chapter. You can do so, too. That is, you can make sure to distinguish what is yours and what is AI. You may not need to go to the extreme and provide proof of your work on the level that you provide a replay of how you craft your documents (see Fernandes and McIntyre, 2025), but your readers should have a clear understanding of what is yours and what comes from your use of AI.

Yet, even still, there are other ethical considerations we must account for when it comes to AI beyond just issues of plagiarism. Indeed, because of the lack of transparency by AI companies, we should be critical of their tools and not only be aware of the injustices they perpetuate but also actively challenge them.

Scholars who study LLMs, for instance, have documented their lack of language diversity. Antonio Byrd (2023) warns of the racism that occurs in the way LLMs are trained, stating:

> ...scholars and teachers in writing studies recognize the rhetorical context and histories of linguistic ideologies and dominant power that have oppressed, mitigated, and erased marginalized communities that LLMs have encoded. Linguistic punishment includes violence against bodies and land: colonialism, imperialism, genocide, and slavery paved the way for English dominance in contemporary global economies. The downstream impact can be felt in corpus text creation.
>
> *(p. 136)*

In other words, if an LLM is trained on already existing racist language, then it will likely provide racist outputs. RCWS scholars have time and again fought to ensure students have a right to their own languages and have sought methods for mitigating oppressive linguistic structures in our classrooms and more broadly in our social settings. Researchers have found, however, that while LLMs can help learners navigate language learning, these AIs can also create new biases in language use and strip writing of the unique idiosyncratic choices that make up our voice (Yakura et al., 2025).

Across disciplines, scholars point to a much larger less-than-wholesome picture of AI, taking into account all that makes up AI from the many (and often expensive) materials used to make them to the biased and marginalizing political and cultural systems that are reinforced by AI. For example, communication and technology scholar Kate Crawford (2021) writes:

> ...artificial intelligence is both embodied and material, made from natural resources, fuel, human labor, infrastructures, logistics, histories, and classifications. AI systems are not autonomous, rational, or able to discern anything without extensive, computationally intensive training with large datasets or predefined rules and rewards. In fact, artificial intelligence as we know it depends entirely on a much wider set of political and social structures. And due to the capital required to build AI at scale and the ways of seeing it optimizes AI systems are ultimately designed to serve existing dominant interests. In this sense, artificial intelligence is a registry of power.
>
> *(p. 8)*

As educators, we often see how tools in our classrooms privilege some while marginalizing others. AI seems to be no different in that regard. In their report on the effects of AI in developing countries, when it comes to education, Mannuru et al. (2023) contend that "negative implications of generative AI in higher education and learning" include "AI homogenizing writing styles and stifling individual expression by prioritizing conformity over originality" and "Raising equity and access concerns, as students lacking necessary technology, infrastructure, or training may face further marginalization" (p. 1043).

Because faculty write documents that matter to their careers, human agency has to factor into the design process, as has been touted so far in this book. To that end, don't let your voice disappear or be overshadowed by AI tools. Be critical of them and the outputs they produce. When your documents serve as means for better work-life balance, classroom practices, fair labor contracts, access to resources, and the like, your voice should shine through. That is what helps keep you human in the eyes of your administration. You are not just a number, a faceless employee. You are a human who cares about your job and making the most of it. The documents you create in academia should help further this cause.

In addition to reflecting on the outputs AI tools provide, you should also think about your role in training AI tools. There are ethical consequences of inputting data into AI tools, whether that is your own data or someone else's. For instance, if we return to the example provided earlier in this chapter of writing a white paper for your department, likely you would have gathered data from and about your colleagues and from students who would potentially enroll in the interdisciplinary course. If you input these data into an AI tool, what else will the AI tool use it for and is that fair to your colleagues and students? Some scholars point to a strategy called participatory training, meaning that "communities and publics beyond technical designers have knowledge, expertise and interests that are essential to the development of AI that aims to strengthen justice and prosperity" (Birhane et al., 2022, p. 7). This approach has the potential to mitigate an AI tool's biases. As Birhane et al. explain, "whether we use participation for algorithmic improvement, methodological innovation, or collective exploration, [these practices] can be characterised along axes of empowerment and reflexive assessment, along which we seek to move away from transactional engagements towards forms of vibrant participation that are in constant engagement with their publics and increase community knowledge and empowerment" (p. 7).

Finally, you might also create documents that may necessitate that others use AI. For example, in your classrooms, you may be asked by your university to develop ways in which to integrate AI into your curriculum. Be aware that not all students have strong technological literacies and may feel excluded if your AI practices are not accessible.

2.8 Reflecting with and on AI

Although you have been prompted throughout this chapter to reflect on AI, it is important to reiterate just how imperative reflection is when using AI tools. Reflection requires self-awareness, and it is this self-awareness that ultimately betters our designs. Before AI, when we used reflection in the past to think about our writing, we concentrated on looking backward, asking ourselves, "What happened and how can I learn from this?" Now, with AI, we still need to look backward, but we also need to look forward and ask ourselves, "What will happen, and how will I learn from it?" In other words, reflecting means looking backward and forward. This is how we can maximize our use of AI.

It is also worth noting that reflection in the moment and reflection of the moment are two different ways that we could look back and look forward, but also is a way to think about the present. When using AI in the moment, we can pause and reflect on what is currently happening to best make a plan for what is next to come.

We can also use AI to instigate our reflection by prompting it to analyze our writing and our ideas as we develop them. Using the output it generates, we can make different decisions and consider additional possibilities for our work. We can generate different perspectives from a range of audiences or ask for questions that can help us get started. Active reflection with AI is a vital part of the intellectual labor embedded in the human work strategy and the HITL model.

2.9 Chapter 2 Review

This chapter focused on what it means to use AI tools to construct documents. Specifically, you learned:

- AI, and particularly GenAI, demands human work and self-awareness;
- AI doesn't "think" or "reflect" like humans do; rather it analyzes patterns in a set of data to produce the most probable output for the prompt you give it. Therefore, it is never 100% accurate;
- the process of writing with AI tools to produce your documents will require rhetorical reflection time and again as you understand, design, research, and revise;
- knowing the affordances and constraints of AI tools can position you to make smarter decisions about designing your documents;
- it is imperative to consider the ethical implications of your use of AI tools;
- using AI calls for reflection in multiple ways.

References

Birhane, Abeba, Isaac, William, Prabhakaran, Vinodkumar, Diaz, Mark, Elish, Madeleine Clare, & Gabriel, Iason. (2022). Power to the people? Opportunities and challenges for participatory AI. *Proceedings of the 2nd ACM Conference on Equity and Access in Algorithms, Mechanisms, and Optimization (EAAMO'22)*, Arlington, VA, article no. 6, Association for Computing Machinery, 1–8. https://doi.org/10.1145/3551624.3555290

Byrd, Antonio. (2023). Truth-telling: Critical inquires on LLMs and the corpus texts that train them. *Composition Studies*, *51*(1), 135–142.

Crawford, Kate. (2021). *Atlas of AI: Power, Politics, and the Planetary Costs of Artificial Intelligence*. Yale University Press.

Fernandes, Maggie, & McIntyre, Megan. (2025) Drafting defensively, documenting authorship: An analysis of Draftback and Grammarly authorship. *Computers and Composition*, *76*, 1–13.

Mannuru, Nishith Reddy, Shahriar, Sakib, Teel, Zoë A., Wang, Ting, Lund, Brady D., Tijani, Solomon, Pohboon, Chalermchai Oak, Agbaji, Daniel, Alhassan, Joy, Galley, Ja Klyn, Kousari, Raana, Ogbadu-Oladapo, Lydia, Saurav, Shubham Kumar, Srivastava, Aishwarya, Tummuru, Sai Priya, Uppala, Sravya, and Vaidya, Praveenkumar. (2023). Artificial intelligence in developing countries: The impact of generative artificial intelligence (AI) technologies for development. *Information Development*, *41*(3), 1036–1054. https://doi.org/10.1177/02666669231200628

Microsoft. (2025, December 15). *Copilot* [Large Language Model]. https://copilot.microsoft.com/

Sylvia IV, J.J., & Reeves, Carol. (2024) Beyond the robot tropes: Embracing nuance and context in the adoption of generative AI. *Journal of Technical Writing and Communication*, *54*(4), 359–368.

United Nations Environment Programme. (2024, September). *AI has an environmental problem. Here's what the world can do about that.* United Nations Environment Assembly. https://www.unep.org/news-and-stories/story/ai-has-environmental-problem-heres-what-world-can-do-about

Vee, Annette. (2023). Large Language Models write answers. *Composition Studies*, *51*(1), 176–181.

Yakura, Hiromu, Lopez-Lopez, Ezequiel, Brinkmann, Levin, Serna, Ignacio, Gupta, Prateek, Soraperra, Ivan, & Rahwan, Iyad. (2025, July). Empirical evidence of Large Language Model's influence on human spoken communication (v3). *Computers and Society*. https://arxiv.org/pdf/2409.01754

3

INFORMATION ARCHITECTURE AND DOCUMENT DESIGN

3.1 Understanding Information

To better our understanding of how, when, and where we design documents, and for whom we design them, we can take the concept of information architecture and apply lateral thinking to it to maximize our design's possibilities. Doing so can enable us to see texts from different perspectives and help us understand how information is shaped, disseminated, and understood across contexts, and how we might better represent who we are and what we do. As we mentioned previously, there are many facets to designing texts. Using empathy, for instance, helps us develop a dynamic understanding of our designs' audiences. From empathy, we can define our problem and then ideate solutions, thinking about all the possibilities for our designs that we can later prototype and test. But, to do any of this, we need some way of organizing or structuring information in ways we and others can understand. Even when it comes to lateral thinking, when we are brainstorming even the most creative and nonsensical ideas, we need some way to grasp what it is we are thinking and communicating. This is when we can rely strategically on information architecture.

While we drew primarily from RCWS scholars earlier in this book, in this chapter we integrate scholarship from researchers working at the intersection of architecture, informatics, and user experience (UX) to expand our understanding of document design and design thinking. Such an approach taps into rhetorical history, highlighting practitioners' abilities to see texts as having writers and audiences working within particular contexts for specific purposes, and prioritizes humans communicating within a situation.

DOI: 10.4324/9781003717232-5

When our documents lack some form of information architecture, they can become frustrating to those who wish to use them. Think back to a time when you tried to use a document, but because of its design you were unable to do so. You likely spent more time than you should have trying to make sense of the document or trying to locate what you came to the document for in the first place. You may have even tried to revise the document in your mind to help you work with it in a meaningful way. And, if you gave up, you are not alone. Documents that lack information architecture are taxing and are likely the result of a breakdown in rhetorical thinking.

Unfortunately, this same scenario plays out in professional settings, including in academia. We often see breakdowns in rhetorical thinking that then lead to frustrating designs. Students, for instance, are told they are bad at reading or don't comprehend complex information well. However, as it turns out, they are working with documents that are not designed with them in mind. As you will see in this chapter, responsible and effective design considers an information architecture that serves its users in ways that are recognizable and rhetorically aware.

3.2 Architecture

The term "architecture" wasn't used in a modern sense until the 1560s. Originally, it meant "the art of building," something we associate architecture with today. However, today, we are also likely to think of it as much as a science as we are to think of it as an art. Framing architecture as a science, we may think about the mathematics required in the measurements, the climatology informing where and how we build, or the technology used to create durable materials. The science of architecture ensures elements of the build such as support beam alignment, level groundwork, and a foundation's bearing capacity. For a structure to last, it must be built with precision.

Framing architecture as an art likely calls to mind the way a structure looks and the message it sends—its aesthetic appeal, its style. We might choose a particular shape for the roof, oval instead of square windows, two French doors instead of one sliding barn door. Because of the dynamic relationship between pragmatism and expression, between science and art, architecture requires balance and consideration. A building that looks good must also be precisely built in order to remain standing.

When we think of architecture today, we may also associate it with other terms that encompass the process of creating a structure from start to finish, both nouns and verbs alike, such as form, foundation, and façade and planning, constructing, and designing. We may even visualize an architect as someone sitting at a drawing desk designing blueprints with a scale ruler and pencils or someone on a construction site wearing a hard hat and directing a crew on where to put up a wall.

Moreover, we likely think of architecture (and architects) beyond the scope of a single physical structure. We may call to mind environmental, sustainability, or green design architecture; or computing multicore architecture or microarchitecture; or storyworld architecture. In *Convergence: The Redesign of Design*, Randy Deutsch (2017) defines **architecture** as "a complex undertaking requiring the input of many individuals with varying interests, backgrounds, and expertise," an undertaking that must account for the recent convergence of processes, tools, technologies, techniques, and means for communication that bring people and machines together (p. 10). He argues that architecture today has evolved to be unlike architecture of years past due in part to this convergence. As he explains, changes in technologies have accelerated our processes for building, which in turn has accelerated the demands of architects.

We argue that writing is at a similar juncture today in that we too must account for the convergences that have taken place among people, actions, contexts, materials, and tools. Everyone is a writer today and will continue to be a writer tomorrow, despite those who claim AI will replace human writing. No doubt writers' roles have changed throughout history with the evolution of technologies, and yet, in this moment, with the rapid development of AI tools, there is still great promise for your role in designing documents responsive to their content, context, and purpose that meet your needs and those of your audience(s).

3.3 Information Architecture and Convergence

In the context of technology and society, convergence is the idea that different technological advancements and societal trends will eventually merge or come together. Convergences of people, technologies, and texts have indeed changed the ways in which we build and disseminate texts in a world that is increasingly telling us we must move faster and work smarter. Largely dependent on information, one goal of convergence theory is to describe and predict how disparate technological fields and societal domains (e.g., media, communications, biotechnology, and computing) come together to create new paradigms or integrated systems. One way to conceptualize this is to consider AI's convergence, which includes humans bringing together a number of technologies (algorithms, hardware, language, etc.) and various human- and machine-generated data (information) to meet the demands of particular environments. As we mentioned earlier, AI technology sorts data, learns from it, seeks patterns within it, and then produces outputs based on this information for its users.

With this in mind, we want to turn now to how we can move forward with document writing and design in this moment of technological and social convergence. We believe that one way to do so is to think more carefully about how we structure and build information. Richard Saul Wurman (1996) popularized the term **information architecture**, explaining it as the art and science of making information clear. In *Information Architecture: For the Web and Beyond*, Louis Rosenfeld, Peter Morville, and Jorge Arango (2015) define information architecture as "the structural design of shared information environments," pointing to the way information is organized, structured, and made accessible within a system or space that multiple people use (p. 24). Given the priority this definition places on joining together people and their environments, we can begin to see how design thinking, and particular convergences, comes into play.

Not every environment is equally conducive to communication. Simply sharing a space with others doesn't guarantee effective or efficient communication. Moreover, different environments may require different ways of communicating. Because of this, document designers should use information architecture. The ultimate goal of information architecture is **usability**. It aims to structure content in ways that make information accessible. In the context of writing, information architecture is like the blueprint or structure of a document, website, or content system. It's about how the information is organized, arranged, and made easy for readers to navigate, just like how a writer organizes their sentences and paragraphs in a clear and logical manner. When we talk about information architecture in relation to writing, we're concerned with how readers navigate and find information, much like how writers use headings, subheadings, and bullet points to make the content easy to digest. In other words, information architecture is "the art and science of shaping information products and experiences to support usability, findability, and understanding" (Rosenfeld, Morville, and Arango, p. 24). Information must flow. There must be an effective exchange or transfer of information among people, processes, and systems that make up environments. Without information flow and without an effective exchange, the environment may lead to confusion, frustration, and miscommunication.

More specifically, information architecture is about designing an environment where all users can easily find, understand, and interact with information in a way that makes the most sense and serves the needs of all those within. Applying information architecture may, for example, involve using taxonomy, metadata, navigation, and usability principles to help everyone understand, but it also means ensuring a coherent and effective structure. In their book, Rosenfeld, Morville, and Arango use examples of digital technologies to point out how designers can categorize and present information in accessible ways and how using cohesive and consistent systems enables a user's understanding of information.

Using Rosenfeld, Morville, and Arango's structure, Figure 3.1 depicts information architecture's four primary concepts. The outer ring in the image includes **organization**, **labeling**, **navigation**, and **findability**. The inner ring of the image briefly identifies how each function may help those who seek to communicate and understand information in an environment. These are the four keys of information use that a designer needs to account for. For instance, if we wish to represent organized information, we may label it using keywords that are familiar to our audiences. Then, to help our audience find what they are looking for when they interact with our text, we may build search and navigation functions into our design. We know that not all our users will experience our texts in exactly the same way; therefore, drawing from rhetorical foundations and design thinking, we can see how thinking about developing an empathetic and grounded understanding of our audiences, our contexts, and our purposes can allow us to build effective, accessible texts.

To capture information architecture and design thinking's convergence in our methodology and to acknowledge Industry 4.0's impact on document writing and design, we add to the concepts of information

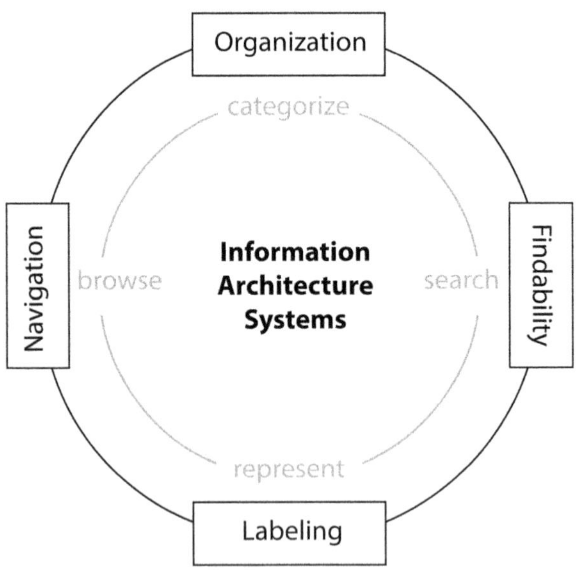

FIGURE 3.1 What information architecture does.

This image depicts how each of the four concepts of organization, labeling, navigation, and search work to build an accessible text.

architecture the values of **flexibility, clarity, integration,** and **scalability** (see Table 3.1 for definitions). Examples in previous chapters demonstrate some of the ways that faculty are often tasked with writing and designing texts that categorize, label, and present information that is not always easy to organize. Our administration may tell us, for instance, that we need to categorize our work in specific ways as we apply for new positions, promotions, and raises. They may give us the categories and tell us specific instructions on how to present our work activities that may or may not align with the work we've done. Including flexibility, clarity, and integration in these design situations can help us better situate the dynamic work we do as academics and help us achieve our goal (see 1.4 Scenario: Categorizing Your Work). Unfortunately, many of the documents we are asked to create, especially those prescribed to us, have become outdated and haven't kept up with the changing nature of our jobs or our implementation of technological advancements. When we consider scalability in our information architecture and document design, we are given a chance to find a range of opportunities for our information structures and documentation. Scalability can lead designers to insights related to circulation and longevity, technology integration, and the information we wish to share. Later in this chapter, we will discuss how we can address these situations using lateral thinking.

For now, let us think a bit more about the primary concepts of information architecture and how we got to this moment in time where the convergence of people, texts, and systems has shaped our designs in diverse ways. After defining information architecture, Rosenfeld, Morville, and Arango explain how the history and evolution of technologies have greatly shaped our interaction with information. They point out that information that was once dependent on (or only found in) one place has now become more independent, thanks to newer technologies. For instance, we no longer have to get a song from one source, like a record, as we can get that same song from multiple technology applications, such as Apple iTunes, Amazon Music, Sirius XM radio, or Spotify, across a multitude of devices, an iPhone, a car's radio, a computer. We can search for that one song in many different ways too, by an artist's name, by song title, by genre. And everyone can access that same song in their own way.

In academia 30 years ago, an assignment's instructions may have been found only in a textbook. Today, instructions may still be located in a textbook, but they may also be found through other technologies. An instructor may post the instructions on a course management site as an online assignment or record herself on video explaining these instructions and post them to a class blog. In addition, students have multiple ways in which they can access them, for instance, with the use of a screen reader or with a range of mobile devices. From the song on a computer to instructions on a blog, what makes these examples possible has to do with information architecture and its ability to make the information (the song and instructions) accessible to all. In each case, information architecture worked and users (listeners and students) were able to get what they came to the environment for.

Before elaborating more on effective information architecture, we want to point out that although information architecture can be applied to digital and nondigital technologies and texts alike, as many of this chapter's examples allude to, it can also be applied to systems themselves. If we think of a library, for instance, the books in it are categorized by a system, such as the one developed by the Library of Congress. That system uses subject, author, and title so that readers can quickly locate what they need not just through an online library database, but on the library's physical shelves. Without a clear system in place, searching for books on a shelf would be a frustrating, inefficient scavenger hunt for library patrons.

WHAT AI HAS TO SAY:

Information architecture is the practice of organizing, structuring, and labeling information so that people can find and use it effectively. In short, it's about making complex information environments—like websites, apps, databases, or even physical spaces—usable and understandable. Richard Saul Wurman, an architect and graphic designer, used it to describe the act of designing the structure of information so people can make sense of it. He argued that just as architects design buildings for human use, information architects design systems of knowledge for human understanding.

Since then, information architecture has become an interdisciplinary field that pulls from:

- Library and information science
    - classification, indexing, and retrieval methods.
- Computer science
    - database design, content management, and human–computer interaction.
- Design and UX
    - navigation, interaction design, and visual hierarchy.
- Communication and rhetoric
    - shaping meaning, audience awareness, and context-sensitive messaging.

What makes Wurman's take powerful is the bridge: information architecture isn't just about technology or aesthetics—it's about human-centered meaning-making. Effective information architecture translates messy or overwhelming data into usable pathways, helping users orient themselves, find what they need, and trust the system.

Code Credit: OpenAI, *ChatGPT* (2025, December 4)

This output may fail to consider how the structure of information can alter meaning. Our culture and experience influence how we receive information and how we make meaning. Even the most effective designs are unlikely going to be accessible to all users.

In citing Wurman, this output presents a Eurocentric perspective of information architecture that might exclude cultures that rely on non-hierarchal or linear ways of knowing.

Example of an AI output using the prompt: "In three paragraphs, explain what information architecture is. Make sure to include examples." Code Credit: OpenAI, *ChatGPT* (2025, December 4).

The AI output in the "What AI Has to Say" example reflects a Western approach to information architecture and implies that meaning-making must be orderly. The output suggests that information must proceed in a universal, hierarchical, and linear manner if it is to be understood. It must be organized. It must be structured. It must be labeled. Otherwise, meaning isn't possible. However, information and the way we understand it is not always a product of organization. It can also be a process of knowing that is inextricably tied to our histories and cultures and the complex (often messy) relationships between them. Inclusive information architecture is not about arranging products and their ideas. It is about acknowledging and then representing the different ways of knowing. And, importantly, to do so authentically through our designs. In inclusive information architecture, we might ask "How does this document's design support users' lived experiences?" and "Whose ways of knowing does my document's design privilege or erase?" In other words, information architecture is contextual; it reflects real and diverse ways of knowing that are grounded in time and place.

The way you organize and label information in your document should be looked at from a historical and cultural lens. Information architecture and the structures we build are not neutral things after all, and they should derive from practices that best serve the information and *all* its users. Not doing so privileges some users over others. Using an example that we will talk about throughout this book can demonstrate such a point. Faculty who are evaluated for performance may be asked to structure their professional document in a linear and compartmentalized way, using labels such as teaching, research, and service, and to do so in that order. This is supposedly to help the administrative evaluators who read the document clearly see that faculty have checked all the boxes, that they have done measurable things in three valued categories, and whether they should be promoted. Yet, for faculty whose work is not easily defined by these labels, such a structure could be frustratingly misrepresentative. The structure, in other words, fails to consider other ways of knowing and representing.

To put it differently, when structuring our documents, we need to prioritize equity. This means purposefully and critically acknowledging whose ways of knowing and whose ways of representing are reflected in our information designs. Equitable information architecture means making sure no one has to render themselves into a different person to use our structures. It means inviting users to access information in a range of ways rather than isolating access and making them feel unwelcome.

3.4 Effective Information Architecture

We encounter information architecture in both digital and nondigital spaces, and many of us use it without really being aware that we're doing so. In nondigital spaces, within, for instance, the physical printed pages of a CV or syllabus, information architecture works to provide readers a clear reading path in which to navigate and understand the information on the document. In other words, it provides a structure or organizational scheme that guides your readers through the document in a way that helps their understanding in addition to giving them clues as to how they should interpret the information. A subheading near the beginning of a CV such as "service" shows readers that you value service and that the experiences written under such a heading are service-related experiences.

In digital spaces, information architecture ensures that users don't get lost in a maze of content. A common example of information architecture in action is a university's website. Let's say you are applying for a teaching position at a particular university. When you visit the homepage of that university's website to find out more about their core values and programs, you might see hyperlinked categories like "Academics," "Athletics," and "Admissions," each leading to subcategories such as "Colleges," "Teams," or "Application Materials." These hyperlinks allow you to narrow your search by a particular academic unit, sport, forms, and so on. A search bar also helps you find specific items directly. For instance, you could type in your discipline or related field and hope that the university's website returns search results that contain these words. If the website utilizes effective information architecture practices, then you will likely get the results you want.

Effective information architecture practices can lead you to better designs. The website's elements (the headings, the hyperlinks, the search bar) should work together to create a seamless system and user experience. Without a search bar, you might resort to seeking out disciplinary-related programs and news through a series of clicks in navigation menus. As you move through pages of information, you may fail to find what you need, leaving you frustrated and confused. In other words, the system would fail you. To prevent such failures, website designers think rhetorically as they carefully plan menus, navigation paths, and search functionalities to ensure everything feels intuitive.

Beyond websites, information architecture plays a role in everyday life, making sure to consider users' expectations. A grocery store, for example, follows information architecture principles by grouping similar products together—produce in one area, dairy in another, and frozen foods in a separate aisle. Imagine if bread were scattered randomly throughout the store instead of being placed in the bakery section. Shoppers would waste time wandering each aisle trying to find a baguette.

The same applies to spaces in our documents—without clear categories, labels, and pathways, readers would have to work much harder to find what they need. Good information architecture simplifies complex information, making systems work for people rather than the other way around. Therefore, information architecture serves as the fourth pillar of document design, the first three pillars being rhetorical reflection, design thinking, and technology use. This fourth pillar marries the "what" with the "how" of designing documents, and to illustrate, Table 3.1 shows what the elements of an effective information architecture are and what they look like in action.

TABLE 3.1 Values of Effective Information Architecture

Value	*Definition*	*Examples*
Flexibility	It is the adaptability of content and application. In other words, it is the *what* and the *how* of our communication. These two cannot be separated as the *how* is just as much a part of meaning-making as the *what.*	A bold font for a phrase or word can signal to the audience that the information is important.
Clarity	It means to provide access to information through recognizable pathways. In other words, it is how we and our readers navigate the communication. These pathways are created when we organize and design elements that guide us through a text.	A hyperlink guides users of a web text to specific additional information.
Integration	This happens when a text effectively brings together multiple modes of communication.	When a text combines visuals, words, audio, and so forth.
Scalability	This is the potential for information spread (circulation), sustainability (longevity), and tech integration.	Sharing a text through a digital networked platform via a certain file type.

These elements have a dynamic relationship with one another; even though we have them separated in Table 3.1, all the elements must work together. They each *require* information and, at the same time, *create* information for ourselves (as the designer) and our audiences (as the users). Acknowledging Marshall McLuhan's (1964) "the medium is the message," we can see that the design itself provides information. For instance, in information architecture, content refers to the existing information we want to share with others as well as the information we create when designing our texts. In other words, we may have some content already in mind when we start to write, but then we might develop the rest as we go along in our attempt to create a systematic way in which our readers can understand our information. We may have pieces of information for a CV already in mind, for instance, as we put together our application for a teaching position. But, we may need to add in or create new information once we start researching that position and the hiring university. When we begin adding to the existing CV, it becomes a new document with new information, new headings, a new organization, and/or a new layout. The look of this new CV tells readers something different from previous versions of our CV.

Effective information architecture is also flexible, which could seem a bit strange given our ideas about an architectural structure's permanence, which often conjures up notions of strength and stability. Who wants to live in a building with a flexible foundation? Something like that sounds as if it might crumble to the ground. But even the strongest of structures have suppleness to them to account for their environments. The Gateway Arch in St. Louis, Missouri, is an example of such an extraordinary architectural feat—at 630 feet tall, the arch is designed to move in order to withstand high winds and earthquakes. It sways several inches in either direction to accommodate its environment without sacrificing its integrity.

Good information architecture must be designed to adapt, and we must be able to revise it for the better. These actions can happen in a number of ways. The adding or changing of a design and of information may happen when we try a new label or organize a piece of information in a certain way in order to tell our readers which information is important, or how information is interrelated. If we bold headings on our syllabus, for example, students know

TABLE 3.2 Activity: Information Scavenger Hunt

CVs require material evidence of work accomplished, awards, accolades, and special activities. After quickly brainstorming a few events and accomplishments, conduct a scavenger hunt in your information environment. Here are some ways of doing this search:

- Examine your email accounts for conference and publication acceptances, agendas and schedules, and award specifics.
- Conduct a search through popular search engines and scholarly databases for events, mentions, publications, acknowledgments, and recognitions.
- Look through your annual job reviews, portfolios, and progress reports for evidence of efficacy and accomplishments.
- Analyze evaluations and classwork for performances that demonstrate abilities and areas for improvement.
- Speak to your peers to find out what they would expect to find on your CV.
- Consider searching other environments for additional materials relevant to your CV.

Once you have completed the scavenger hunt, take the gathered information and create a CV with it, thinking carefully about the different ways you can organize and structure it in a way that will help your readers navigate.

that they are starting a new section and information included in that section likely corresponds to the subject identified in the section heading. Readers also now understand that they should make note of the relationship between that section's content and other sections in the syllabus.

Information architecture plays a crucial role in designing documents by ensuring that content is structured, organized, and easy to navigate. Without a strong information architecture foundation, documents can feel cluttered, making it difficult for readers to extract key information efficiently. Just like a well-designed website, a document should present information logically so that readers can quickly find what they need without feeling overwhelmed. This could involve clear headings, subheadings, bullet points, and an intuitive layout that guides the reader naturally through the content. In addition, good information architecture design can build a coherent narrative of the writer and their content as the reader moves through a document. An example of this would be when a website's navigation points users to prioritized information, which helps paint a clear picture for users. In other words, good information architecture helps build a good story that meets the demands of the situation, including ensuring accessibility for readers.

To demonstrate, in a syllabus, information architecture can help structure content by breaking it into sections. Using numbered headings and subheadings allows students to jump to relevant sections without scrolling aimlessly. Visual elements like tables further enhance readability by presenting complex information in an accessible way. A good design of the syllabus tells a

TABLE 3.3 Activity: New Class Syllabus

Consider creating a syllabus for a new class that focuses on AI in your discipline. The course requires students to theorize AI technology and why they should use it ethically. It also requires students to apply new techniques and strategies for appropriately using a variety of AI technologies. Imagine how you might design the syllabus for this class. Use the following lists to sketch out the necessary information you need to communicate to students, the section headings and subheadings needed to organize this information, and any design elements that will help your students understand the information. Finally, consider how your organization and structure help tell a story to your students about the course.

The course learning outcomes are:

- analyze AI technologies and tools in various contexts
- define and apply critical thinking skills
- create professional deliverables for various audiences with AI
- identify appropriate and ethical strategies for implementing AI

Necessary Information	Headings and Subheadings	Design Elements

particular story to the students about the course. A poorly organized syllabus, on the other hand, might bury important information in long paragraphs with no clear hierarchy, forcing students to sift through unnecessary details.

Even documents like grant proposals and curriculum assessments benefit from good information architecture. Distinct sections for goals, outcomes, procedures, and a budget in a grant proposal help granting committees quickly assess the merits of the proposal. Similarly, a well-structured curriculum assessment document that uses bolded keywords, step-by-step instructions for conducting the assessment, and numbered outcomes of the assessment makes it easier for administrators and faculty to assess whether the curriculum is succeeding. In both cases, information architecture ensures that the document isn't just a block of text, but a well-organized tool designed for clarity and usability. As a result, readers are likely to navigate through the document smoothly.

3.5 Information Architecture and Lateral Thinking

By now, it might be evident to you that linear thinking is a key part of information architecture. As we described in Chapter 1, linear thinking involves a straightforward, logical, and systematic approach, which many of the examples in this chapter show. Using logical elements such as categories, steps, and sections to organize information certainly engages linear thinking.

However, and this is a *big* however, linear thinking, as we have pointed out, doesn't always serve us well or serve everyone in our audiences. It may flatten our work as we saw in Chapter 1. It may lead to misrepresenting the information, content, or even us, the document's creator. It may be too rigid, too structured, too restrictive. It may rely on genre conventions that are exclusionary or old institutional procedures that haven't kept up with changing times or the diverse people who work and learn within academia. It may assume all users of our information navigate and understand information in the same ways. To be more accommodating in our designs, we can turn now to lateral thinking to help create dynamic user experiences with information architecture.

Lateral thinking is a problem-solving approach that involves looking at a situation from an unconventional or creative perspective. It contrasts with logical or linear thinking as previously mentioned, namely, because it encourages thinking outside of the box, challenging assumptions, and approaching problems in innovative ways. When the concept was introduced by Edward de Bono in 1967, he emphasized that lateral thinking is about changing patterns, restructuring ideas, and finding new connections rather than just following traditional logic.

Information architecture plus lateral thinking encourages us to think of documents more dynamically and creatively. But, most importantly, using both helps us maintain our authenticity and individuality (that self-awareness we discussed earlier in this book). While linear thinking benefits document design and production in that it helps us organize within the constraints of media, thinking across documents and information streams and beyond genre conventions and categories—or lateral thinking—can help us reposition the work we do, change the ways in which we communicate it, and find new means through which to develop and deliver documents. In other words, lateral thinking can encourage us to consider how information converges to best work for us and our document's users.

TABLE 3.4 Remix: Information Scavenger Hunt

Look back to Table 3.2: Activity: Information Scavenger Hunt and rework the CV you created, trying different designs to organize, label, construct, and present the information you gathered. For example, create a new CV for a teaching institution, a new CV for a research institution, and an alternative academic position (i.e., working as a grant writer, working for an assessment office). As you do this, think about creative ways of designing your CV that takes into consideration lateral thinking.
Now, show your different versions of yours to your peers, garner feedback, and revise to strengthen your writing.

As we have already discussed, it is often difficult to categorize the work we do in distinct domains like teaching, research, and service. When we are confined to linear texts, such as PDFs, webpages, or physical pages, this challenge is further complicated. Using information architecture more effectively through lateral thinking, then, can help us unflatten our work and to think of it more inclusively. This is important as the nature of what we do changes. Faculty are often asked to wear many hats on their campuses, such as run college-wide programs, assess programs or colleagues, facilitate student and faculty workshops, manage university sites, lead committees, generate public-facing materials, liaise with multiple disciplines, and so on. Many faculty spend their careers doing things that can be hard to define neatly. Therefore, as dynamic professionals, faculty must be willing to adapt to changing contexts and learning on the go, and so too must their texts.

Applying lateral thinking with information architecture means that we can think creatively even when facing circumstances that feel frustratingly confined or rigid. When designing our CV, we might, for example, use declarative statements instead of traditional section headings like teaching and research. We might label sections "Application of Research in the Classroom" and "Application of Research in the Community" to show that we are teachers and researchers, and to show that our research impacts different audiences and environments and shouldn't necessarily be separated from the who, where, and why of our work. Likewise, perhaps, we want a more dynamic CV, one that can be read in different ways. We might create an interactive video that allows viewers to "jump" to themes like multimodality and literacy or historic preservation and urban planning so they can watch our work in action. Or, we might create an online CV with images that represent the convergences of the work we do. When we submit the "paperwork," we may simply turn in a URL.

TABLE 3.5 Activity: Analyze a Job Document

Choose a document that you created for a job application or for a class and identify its information architecture—its structure, organization, content, pathways, and circulation systems. Why or how did you choose this structure for the document? How would a different organizational design send a different message? Would removing labels help? Would using images help? Imagine all the possibilities for it and revise the document with an alternative information architecture.

If "being proficient in any one domain—whether skill, technology, or tool—is no longer sufficient," as Deutsch (2017) argues, then articulating our work as singular is no longer sufficient either (p. 217). The act of using information architecture with lateral thinking to unflatten our work and to articulate its dynamicness is in a sense the act of releasing ourselves from traditional institutional categories that are exclusionary. But, how do we do information architecture with lateral thinking?

A good place to start is a place that RCWS faculty encourage their writing students to begin from: brainstorming. **Brainstorming** is an important step when using lateral thinking with information architecture. In fact, during brainstorming, we can be creative by thinking about all possibilities, even those that might seem a bit ridiculous. For example, as you brainstorm ideas for the new AI course in Table 3.3: Activity: New Class Syllabus, you might consider a number of brainstorming activities. One way could be to think in opposites. What is the opposite of digital writing? What does it look like? What can students learn from this kind of writing? In thinking about what digital writing is not or the opposite of, you might be able to see how even nondigital writing is writing nonetheless and still has a rhetorical context in which it is valid. This might be a good idea to discuss with your students in class using examples.

In addition to brainstorming, there are numerous other lateral thinking actions we can use with information architecture. And we can apply them to document design beyond course syllabi. So, what follows then is not an all-encompassing list of such actions, but rather a brief list to help you get started. We believe the best way to engage in each of these actions is to start by answering questions with creative answers. Instead of restricting your answers with genre conventions, try freeing your mind and considering a range of outcomes for your designs. In addition to using the questions in Table 3.6, we also recommend checking out how the actions could apply to a specific text (in this case, a CV).

TABLE 3.6 Lateral Thinking Actions and Examples

Action	*What questions to ask*	*Examples for a CV*
Identify traditional assumptions	What are the common conventions of the genre and why do I need to follow them? What can I do that is different?	Instead of creating a CV that uses a chronological format, you could choose to create an achievement-based or skills-focused CV.
Reframe the problem and solutions	Is there a different way to phrase the problem? Have I considered all angles of the problem? Am I considering all reasons for the problem? What are all possible solutions, even ones that may seem absurd?	Instead of thinking you need a job, consider how you can fill a gap at the university hosting the job ad. They need to hire you specifically, and your unique CV will show that you are the solution.
Reframe the presentation	Does my text need to look like everyone else's text? Is there a look that best represents me? What are all possible designs for my text?	Instead of listing job duties in bullet points, frame your experience in terms of problem-solving and innovation. Use storytelling techniques. Show how you solved challenges, improved processes, or delivered unique value.
Incorporate unconventional elements	How can unconventional elements strengthen my text? What will doing so say about me?	Add a QR code linking to a personal website, video introduction, or portfolio. Use graphs, statistics, or brief project summaries to visually showcase expertise.
Use unexpected analogies	How can I describe my experience in a way that surprises but also makes sense?	Instead of writing this on a CV: "Managed a department of 10 faculty," you might try: "Led a team of 10 faculty like a championship coach, turning our department members into successful colleagues on campus."

(*Continued*)

TABLE 3.6 (Continued)

Action	*What questions to ask*	*Examples for a CV*
Think visually	Do I need only words to express my thoughts? Can I use visuals to better communicate my ideas?	Use icons, progress bars, or mini case studies to break the monotony of text. Use a before-and-after impact graph to show how your methods improved student outcomes.
Choose different language	Is there a better way of saying what I want to say? Can I use language that is unique to me?	Describe your teaching experience as "Turning Classrooms into Learning Labs," showcasing innovative teaching methods.

There are certainly other actions you can take besides those listed in Table 3.6. So, we encourage you to think about your own circumstances and look for ways to be creative in your approaches to designing your texts. In addition, we also believe that you should share these actions with others so that they too can make design decisions that best suit their circumstances.

3.5.1 Pushing Back

Up to this point, we have been working toward a better, more inclusive way of designing texts. Indeed, information architecture with lateral thinking may help us push back against forms, texts, and conventions that exclude people. Throughout our careers in academia, we may find ourselves in a situation where we are told to use designs that don't work for us. This might happen when we are instructed to use forms with conventions that are outdated or exclusionary. Using lateral thinking with information architecture may help us circumnavigate these situations and/or make them work for us rather than against us.

This is an important point that we would like to make here. To provide everyone with an equal opportunity to succeed, the work we do must be represented in texts that best represent us. When we use lateral thinking, we are positioned to account for socioeconomic and cultural differences in how we communicate information that some conventions don't include. The RCWS field has worked to ensure students have a right to their own language. Indeed, our field and our scholarship have made this argument time and again. We believe that faculty and professionals should have a right to their own language too. We are often bound by expectations that long predate our generation and don't necessarily reflect best communication practices (such as not hyperlinking research in a CV or using visuals when we're a visual culture). To that end, let us unlock our potential with lateral thinking to highlight what makes us unique and multidimensional.

Let us consider all possibilities for designing our information in ways that best represents us and to push back against practices that do not. Drawing on rhetorical reflection practices, you are well situated to do this work when applying lateral thinking to information architecture.

Here is just one example of how this can work:

> Let's say that your college offers faculty an opportunity for a course release in the upcoming semester if faculty have a substantial research project they would like to conduct. To be granted this release, faculty must submit a form outlining their research project's purpose, procedures, and expected outcomes, which college leadership will use to assess whether the project warrants a course release. However, because you work in a college where science-based faculty far outnumber humanities, arts, and social sciences faculty, the form is biased toward science research, including prompts that ask faculty to detail experiments and hypotheses and to describe their labs. Your project is a case study on policy and gentrification in an urban neighborhood.

A case study can be a significant research project, but you likely wouldn't use the word "experiment" to describe this kind of research. Thinking laterally about how you can turn a section called "experiment" into a more appropriate research approach in your field, you might reframe this section of your application by using "research site" instead of "lab" so that your description is more recognizable to your audience (i.e., leadership) and more accurately reflects your research. Another lateral move might include using visual markers such as typography or iconography to correlate elements of your research to elements common in science research. For example, rather than simply describing your research site, you might find it more persuasive to include images of your "lab" before and after the policy was enacted. The significant contribution that lateral thinking affords you is the ability to approach the problem from multiple perspectives and find opportunities to push against constraints that don't serve your purpose.

Pushing back is easier said than done, of course, given that many of our institutions have traditional policies in place that are top-down or are beholden to policies that may misalign with our own values. But, the more we use lateral thinking with information architecture, the more capable we are to make known and mitigate exclusionary practices.

3.6 Scenario: Assessing Application Materials

You have been tasked to lead a hiring committee for a faculty position your department wishes to fill. Your job advertisement is published, and you receive 80 applications, each containing a cover letter, CV, sample teaching documents, and a teaching philosophy. To organize and keep track of all the candidates and their information, you devise a system using a spreadsheet. At the top of the spreadsheet, you create labels that include the following: teaching experience, research experience, service experience, and administration experience.

As you and your committee members work your way through the applications and fill in the spreadsheet with notes, you realize that your system may favor certain candidates over others. Likewise, some of the information you are sorting through doesn't neatly fit under any of the labels. In fact, you begin adding more categories, which makes it cumbersome to read, and realize the document has grown too large as a result.

TABLE 3.7 Activity: Reimagining Application Assessment

Using the scenario in Section 3.6, design an assessment system (i.e., rubric, spreadsheet, forms, etc.) that spotlights each candidate's strengths without devaluing their lived experiences and material reality. Consider the following questions to help you begin your information architecture design:

- How do you manage a large amount of information?
- What system elements could you put in place to highlight each candidate's strengths?
- What system elements or categories could you include to ensure the committee's evaluation is inclusive?

Now that you have thought about what it means to handle candidates' information, what can you take away from this experience to shape what you ask of future potential candidates in the application process and what can you do differently to shape your job ad? Consider how your responses change when the categories are *teaching*, *research*, *service*, and *administration*. How does separating, for example, service from administration alter how the work is represented? What alternative approaches might you use to represent the work described in this scenario?

Table 3.7 asks you to apply lateral thinking to information architecture design to prioritize equitable consideration of all applicants.

3.7 Adapting to Opportunity

Information architecture with lateral thinking can provide opportunities to call out conventions that are exclusionary and can help us heighten our awareness and sensitivity to cultural, racial, ethnic, and socioeconomic biases that prevent people from using and understanding texts. These are wicked problems and require us to think creatively about the solutions to them. In the example in Section 3.5.1 about the course release procedure, you are presented with an opportunity to help solve such a wicked problem. But not all wicked problems have an easy solution. Our hope is that while you may feel frustrated initially by the lack of inclusivity that texts may afford you, by using information architecture with lateral thinking you can build a text that still works for you and one that shows how your uniqueness belongs. For example, rather than writing a bullet point about multimodal projects on a CV in a Microsoft Word document, a writing instructor could build a website that showcases their teaching experience by including videos of their students' projects to better show how they value the connection between different modes of communication. In another example, an art instructor conducting research on the best practices for teaching drawing may want to create a video showcasing students drawing in class to demonstrate not just the end product, but the processes students took to create their art.

3.8 Scenario: Writing a Narrative

You've been working at your university as an assistant professor for a few years, and you review the faculty manual's criteria for promotion annually. Your university requires a number of publications or alternative means of circulating research. Your teaching must meet an exceptional standard, evidenced by annual evaluation reports and student letters of support. You must also demonstrate that you have contributed meaningfully to the university and local community through service activities. You believe you finally meet all the requirements and decide you want to apply for associate professor. Among the application requirements is a narrative of the work you have done to earn this promotion.

TABLE 3.8 Activity: Reimagine How You Tell Your Story

Write your narrative in a way that best expresses your experience at your university. Consider what you want to highlight and what that says about the kind of faculty member you have been. How will you describe the work you did? How will you organize this narrative? What kind of text would suit this narrative the best?

Writing a narrative (and documents like it) is about more than making sure you have included all the necessary content or followed the instructions from a faculty handbook. It is about designing a structure that tells a story and guides readers' understanding of it. How will your readers navigate your story and in what ways? While this story should share the work that you have done and the accomplishments you have achieved, remember that your readers will be using this document to evaluate you and your work. What have you done in your structure that can make this job easy for them? What have you done to invite them in? Your document's information architecture will shape how readers perform this job. However, while it is important that you make design decisions that meet your readers' needs, meeting these needs does not mean that you must compromise the story you want to tell. It is possible to craft an impactful story that works for you and for your readers.

3.9 Chapter 3 Review

In this chapter, we introduced applying lateral thinking to information architecture and how doing so can help us think creatively about our designs. Now is a good time to reflect on the following concepts:

- information architecture refers to the convergence of processes, tools, technologies, techniques, and means of communication that bring people and machines together;
- information architecture helps us design documents by ensuring that content is structured, organized, and easy to navigate and find;
- applying lateral thinking to information architecture helps us unflatten our designs and think creatively about solving wicked problems with our designs;
- there are numerous actions to employ information architecture with lateral thinking to push back against exclusionary practices by challenging conventions, reimagining problems, and brainstorming all possibilities.

References

de Bono, Edward. (1967). *The use of lateral thinking*. Jonathan Cape.
Deutsch, Randy. (2017). *Convergence: The redesign of design*. Wiley.
McLuhan, Marshall. (1964). *Understanding media: The extensions of man*. McGraw-Hill.
OpenAI. (2025, December 4). *ChatGPT* (GPT-5) [Large Language Model]. https://chatgpt.com/.
Rosenfeld, Louis, Morville, Peter, & Arango, Jorge. (2015). *Information architecture: For the web and beyond*, 4th ed. O'Reilly Media.
Wurman, Richard Saul. (1996). *Information architects*. Illustrated by Peter Bradford, Graphis Press.

PART II

Designing and [Re] Presenting Your Work

4

DIVERGENT DESIGN

On April 11, 1970, NASA launched its Apollo 13 mission for the moon. Little did they know that what would transpire over the next several days would not only captivate the world but also provide an example of how divergent thinking can solve problems in creative ways. During the mission, an oxygen tank exploded, severely damaging the spacecraft and presenting those working the mission, both in space and back on Earth, with serious problems. Because the spacecraft was no longer capable of returning to Earth, the crew had to adapt the Lunar Module and use that as their means for journeying home. But, the Lunar Module was not meant for such a journey—it didn't have the right power and navigation systems, not enough water, and its carbon dioxide filters wouldn't last long enough to see the crew to safety.

Thinking laterally and imagining the Lunar Module as a lifeboat, NASA quickly came up with as many potential solutions as possible given the constraints of the situation. They needed to figure out, for example, how to adapt the square filters of the Command Module to the Lunar Module's round openings. As the story goes, NASA gathered up the same materials the crew had on board and worked through them from mission control in Houston. They had to improvise by visualizing the objects working together to solve such a problem. On the surface, these objects didn't appear to have much of a relationship with one another other than the fact that they were on the same ship. Yet NASA needed to use them in a

DOI: 10.4324/9781003717232-7

creative way to help the crew adapt the filters to the Lunar Module. Ultimately, they determined that using plastic bags, a cardboard cover from a manual, a sock, a hose, and duct tape would have to suffice. And it did. The crew was able to adapt the filters and use the Lunar Module to make it back to Earth alive.

This story represents the power of divergent design, and although you may not be an astronaut or work for NASA, you will find that you too can harness divergent design when solving your writing problems. Using **divergent design** means using an imaginative and exploratory approach to finding hidden variables, or the [un]knowns of a communicative situation, that can reshape your understanding of your documents and provide you with innovative opportunities for designing them. Divergent design utilizes ideation and lateral thinking, two concepts you learned about in Chapter 1. Just like NASA, you too can develop diverse, nonlinear solutions through experimenting, pushing boundaries, and grappling with the unexpected.

In expanding your possibilities, you diverge from a linear path and consider new directions and perspectives. In Part I of this book, you learned about different phases of document design, one of which was ideation. In this stage, divergent design practices can enable you to brainstorm as many ideas as possible, including the most alternative and creative ideas. In so doing, you have the ability to push the boundaries of different genres, traditional conventions, modes, formats, layouts, and media.

When it comes to documents, divergent design strategies can take on many shapes when you engage in generating ideas for what's possible. For instance, imagine that you are applying for a faculty position and the job application requires you to submit a cover letter. To develop this cover letter, you decide to come up with as many creative possibilities as you can. You think imaginatively, much like NASA did, and you gather up objects that represent your experiences, your abilities, and your goals—a certificate, a favorite pen, a flash drive, a work from your favorite scholar, a conference program—and place them on a table in front of you. You sit and reflect on what you see, making notes and sketching out the stories these objects tell, how they can be pieced together to help you solve your task of writing a cover letter.

In this moment, you are not worried about the end product just yet. It doesn't matter if you will reference all that you see on the table in your letter or if anything you create from those objects is appropriate for the genre. You are more concerned with the opportunities that arise in this creative exercise and how you can pursue them further. What information trails are created through your reflections and considerations of the objects on the table? What does this content reveal about your values, your goals? How does this exercise stretch your understanding, and how might it find its way to your cover letter? This is divergent design.

4.1 GOOD Principles of Divergent Design

While convergent design is about filtering and narrowing (more on this in the next chapter), divergent design is about opening up to uncertainty without settling too soon on one final design. It is about the **rhetorical canons** of **invention** and **arrangement**; ideation, if you will. It is about imagination and looking beyond familiar pathways. However, it should be noted here that while you may begin with invention, we continue to invent throughout the designing of a document as writing is a recursive activity. You might start with one idea that might lead to another; then, after drafting those ideas, yet another idea comes to light. Designing and writing texts is often a messy endeavor; being open to the mess helps us confront texts and conventions that might be exclusionary and work to find solutions for them.

To help you expand your opportunities for writing documents, this chapter presents four **GOOD principles**, or actions, for divergent design. Later, in Chapter 5, you will learn about the CORE principles for convergent design that pair with the GOOD principles of divergent design. Together, the GOOD CORE of divergent and convergent design will help you work through all five of the rhetorical canons. In other words, using them will help you create an effective document from start to finish. Because this book is a linear text, they are presented in a particular order. However, as you will see, as designers, we often move back and forth between them. In addition, we use the term principles loosely. We do not mean for them to be prescriptive or a neutral standard devoid of nuisances. We recognize that there are other ways to achieve your designs. Take them as suggestions but not as complete, universal principles.

The following table, thus, provides examples of GOOD divergent design principles in action, and later, the scenarios that follow will demonstrate how you might apply them. Before the table, though, it should be noted that the term "good" here again should not be read as these are the only good principles available. Rather, based on research and experience, we have found that these have been successful. Likewise, the point of these GOOD principles is to be messy, and messiness can be a good thing in a number of ways, one being that it allows us to not fall into the trap of generic, formulaic writing. It allows us to free our minds to think about all possibilities.

TABLE 4.1 GOOD Principles of Divergent Design

Principle	*What the Principle Means*	*Examples*
Generate abundance	To consider many possibilities without worrying about the quality of them. Think breadth before depth and volume over refinement.	Rapidly prototyping multiple versions of your document.
Originate novel approaches	To consider ways of designing you have never tried before with the goal of broadening your perspective. To be empathetic to others' perspectives.	Seeking input from others or unrelated disciplines, audiences, and stakeholders.
Optimize creative thinking	To consider alternative ways of thinking. Experiment and play to generate novel ideas, considerations, and approaches.	Using perspective manipulation like role-based approaches, or alternate composing mediums like drawings, maps, or sculpture.
Discover the unexpected	To value uncommon, surprising, and startling ideas without writing them off as unusable.	Challenging assumptions through "what if" questions or pattern activities like substitutions and word association.

4.1.1 Generate Abundance

As the name suggests, this principle is about finding all the available means. It is about coming up with as many possible ideas for your document without feeling the urge to delete them right away no matter how far-fetched. Generating abundance can be a liberating creative exercise as it allows you to free yourself from the constraints of expectation and convention. It can also push your brain. For example, one exercise you could use is the popular improvisation exercise, "Yes, and," which encourages participants to seek out "what if" responses that elaborate or develop scenarios, problems, or experiences. Say, for instance, your department will participate in an upcoming open house on campus. The purpose of the open house is for prospective students to learn more about the programs and degrees each department on campus has to offer. Because your department has seen a decline in majors and minors over the past few years, your department chair sees this as a good opportunity to recruit future students and asks you to create a brochure highlighting the major selling points of your department's majors and minors. To help you come up with as many designs for the brochure as possible, you ask several colleagues to join you in answering "Yes, and." You start by suggesting a design concept. Your colleague then builds on this concept by saying "yes" and then offering an additional concept that builds on the original. Then, your next colleague does the same, contributing another concept that builds on both the original concept and the next one. After several rounds of "Yes, and" you have generated an abundance of ideas.

RCWS certainly has a long history of invention strategies that include generating abundance, but it might be more helpful to think here about a common writing assignment in a college classroom, that is, the essay. More modern perspectives of the essay have turned it into something that is prescriptive, formulaic even. Think about the five-paragraph essay, a template for crafting an essay that has an introduction, three body paragraphs, and a conclusion. However, the essay, as originally defined by Montague (1958) in the early 1500s, meant "to try." It was not a clean, straightforward method for writing. Rather it was a space where writers could attempt something. And that is what divergent design as well as generating abundance is about. It is about trying new ideas, attempting something that hasn't been done before.

4.1.2 Originate Novel Approaches

Using the brochure example from the previous section, you might now move to coming up with novel or unique approaches to designing the brochure. You could utilize an exercise in opposites to do so. For instance, what is the opposite of a brochure? To answer this, you might start with what a brochure is. It's something that's promotional and concise; it invites and persuades readers with small chunks of information and key takeaways. A text that would be the opposite of a brochure might be something that is long, analytical, and exhaustive. Say, a report. The form of a brochure is compact and folded. A report is not. A brochure uses marketing language. A report does not. But, if you were to imagine a report of your department's majors and minors, what might it say? And, how could you use this in turn to think more deeply about what might be important to include in your actual brochure?

This exercise of reframing different documents in different genres would be a novel approach given that your task isn't to actually create a report for the open house; rather, it is to create a brochure. Yet, imagining a report as your task and what it might say just might generate additional ideas, some even better, for your actual brochure.

4.1.3 Optimize Creative Thinking

Creativity flows best when we are feeling playful and the stakes are low. But, in academia, creating such a situation can be tricky. When asked to help your department's majors and minors by creating a brochure to recruit new students, you indeed might feel the pressure to succeed. However, there are moves you can make to optimize your creative thinking despite this trickiness. Although not an exhaustive list, the following can provide some ways in which to help you make the most of your creativity.

- Change your scenery. Physically moving out of one space and into another might give you a mental shift to think differently about your document's design. If you can't physically move out of your space, change the space. Cover your walls with sketches, post-its, and storyboards to remind you of different ways of seeing the work you are doing to create a brochure.
- Heighten your mindset. Believe that there are no such things as failed ideas. Every idea is evidence of exploration. Avoid letting yourself judge your ideas.
- Compare in random ways. Compare your design task or intended document with random objects, for example, to help create helpful metaphors that can inspire. How is a brochure like a cassette tape? How is a brochure like a restaurant menu?
- Take on different identities. Imagine being someone else, such as a storyteller, architect, or visionary, to move beyond just being department faculty. What would each of these identities say and do with a brochure? This may even mean that you cross disciplines too. How would an engineer design a brochure? How would a biologist?
- Evoke your senses. Sample different textures, colors, and tones for your designs. Designing isn't just thinking. It's also about feeling, seeing, hearing, and so on.

These creative and exploratory exercises are about shutting down constraints, freeing your mind and body, and giving yourself the best chance to be creative.

4.1.4 Discover the Unexpected

Finally, you might push the opposite exercise from Section 4.1.2 Originate Novel Approaches a bit further to help you see something you were not expecting. Instead of imagining a document like a report as the opposite of a brochure, you could imagine the opposite of the brochure's purpose. The purpose of the brochure is to clarify and simplify information into small concise chunks as well as to entice readers. The opposite of this purpose would be to complicate and question. How, for example, can you complicate and question the information you have about your department's majors and minors? What surprising findings will you discover when you do so?

You could even go so far as to question the purpose of a brochure. What is lost when your department wants to rely on a polished marketing brochure? What would happen if you generated a list of reasons why using a brochure would not be a good idea? Perhaps, this could show you something you hadn't considered before. Perhaps, it will lead you down a different path, one that is most suited to helping you recruit new students.

TABLE 4.2 Using AI to Discover the Unexpected

Choose a document that you are currently working on and ask a GenAI tool to give you reasons why writing this document as opposed to other types of documents would be a bad idea. Next, ask this GenAI tool to help you determine the opposite of the document you are creating and/or the opposite of the document genre's purpose to determine what is lost when designing such a document.
When you receive the output, take a moment and reflect on your findings. What did you learn that you can use moving forward to design a document that is best suited to your and your audience's needs?

4.2 Scenario: Grant Writing Using Lateral Thinking and Divergent Design

Lateral thinking is very much a part of divergent design, but the two are not the same. Lateral thinking also applies to reading and research techniques (lateral reading and lateral source analysis, for example). Divergent design, however, needs lateral thinking and creative thinking. Lateral thinking lets us challenge the status quo, and creative thinking allows us to let go of the status quo entirely. Keeping this in mind, for this scenario, think about a current research project you are working on. If you are not currently working on one, think about research you would like to do in the near future. Now imagine that you are applying for a mid-level grant from a private organization to support this research project. The grant application requires 1) an impact statement, 2) a narrative, 3) a budget, and 4) a timeline. For this scenario, work through the following steps. As you do, notice how you are employing GOOD principles of divergent design through creative writing activities.

First, you need to determine what your research is about and who the research will impact. So, begin by writing out your research problem definition and turn that into several PoV statements. Remember that in Chapter 1, you learned that a PoV statement centers the user(s). Applying divergent thinking, develop several PoV statements for different audiences (e.g., an administrator, a community leader, someone who isn't in your field, a relevant industry professional, and/or an undergraduate student). This can, perhaps, help you consider not just one impact or one audience for your research but multiple.

Second, to begin drafting your narrative, record (via audio or video recorder) yourself telling the story of your research to an academic audience and to a nonacademic audience. Listen to or watch both recordings. What are the similarities and differences you hear in the two recordings? What opportunities reveal themselves as you begin to write your narrative? Use this material to write an early draft of your narrative.

After you have your draft, print it out and cut it up into sentences or paragraphs. Rearrange these and imagine a different ordering of your words and ideas. What other possibilities can you come up with for how your narrative should be told?

If you would like another imaginative way of writing your narrative, meet with a friend or colleague and try to explain your project in two minutes. Then, aim to explain it in less than 60 seconds. When you make it concise, what changes? What did you determine was necessary? What was the listener's general impression of the project? What was unclear to them?

Third, once you have a narrative and an impact statement, turn your attention to the timeline. Find a chalk or whiteboard, draw a horizontal line across the center of it. At one end, mark the start date of your research; at the other end, mark the end date. Now, make notes of the different steps or actions you will take along this line, marking when they will take place and for how long. Take a picture of your timeline. Then, erase all of the items on the board and try imagining a different timeline, one that is stacked, with branches sticking out to the left and right, or one that is circular, with events placed around the edges like a clock and each section of the circle representing a unit of time. Compare your experiences creating these timelines. What do you notice?

If you want an altogether different approach for developing a timeline, grab some sticky notes and begin thinking about all the steps or tasks in the project's workflow. Write each one down on a sticky note, leaving enough room on the note to add the amount of time needed to complete each task. Next, go through each note and estimate the time needed to complete the activity and write that down on the note too. For example, if your project includes interviewing community members, then you'll need an individual note for each of the following actions: drafting the interview protocol, receiving IRB approval, interviewing, and transcribing. Each of these steps takes a different amount of time. You might also have tasks or activities that are time-sensitive. If you're developing a grant that will support travel for a class you're teaching, the dates in which the class runs will contribute significantly to your timeline.

Once you have identified every task involved in completing your project and the time it will take to accomplish them, begin arranging the sticky notes on a wall, window, board, or door—whatever flat surface is available. Arrange your notes according to the amount of time needed to complete each action. This gives you a sense of where most of your effort and time will likely occur in your workflow. Using the activities that will take the longest amount of time to complete, create a "central timeline" by arranging these notes by process, starting with the final step and working backward. Then consider where you can overlap activities and place your sticky notes accordingly (you might stick the less time-consuming overlapping activities to those that will take longer to complete, or place them above or below your "central timeline," or you might need to further deconstruct the more time-consuming activities into additional sticky notes). Once you have your timeline generally in place, you might also consider adding additional details to each note, such as location constraints, costs incurred, or resources needed to complete each step.

Finally, consider your budget. Draw a storyboard of your research scene(s) with colored pencils, making sure to include who is involved, what materials and equipment you will use (and how you will use them), and where you will be doing your research. Then, identify the budget items in this storyboard, noting their costs.

Reflect on these budget items further. What would happen if your research were conducted in a different location using different materials? What would change? For example, say your initial research plan involves studying the impacts of nature writing in national parks by videotaping writers at work. Let's say you can no longer visit these parks and you no longer have access to a video camera. Instead, you turn to local parks and write your observations in a notebook. How would your budget change? How does using technology or no technology impact your budget? Likely, there is a limit to the amount of funding the private organization will grant, but what if you had all the money in the world to conduct this research? What if you had no money at all? How would you approach your research in these instances?

TABLE 4.3 Activity: Using GenAI to Develop a Grant Proposal Budget

To help you discover additional possibilities for the grant proposal budget in the scenario in Section 4.2, consider these divergent design approaches that leverage GenAI.

1. Prompt GenAI with a summary of your narrative and impact statement and ask it to come up with as many grant budget categories as possible (e.g., equipment, travel, supplies, personnel, indirect costs). Then, ask GenAI to consider multiple ways of listing items in each category. What do these multiple pathways tell you about your costs?
2. Ask GenAI to consider different scenarios for the allocation of funding. For example, you could ask it to rebalance your $20,000 budget so that more money goes to personnel or equipment.
3. Ask GenAI to turn your budget into a narrative paragraph or a bulleted list with explanations that justify your use of the funding. How do the different versions help you think about how the funding will be used?

Note: If you use GenAI for a grant in the future, please make sure to adhere to the grant funding organization's policies on AI as most organizations now have policies on the use of AI.

In the early stages of designing an impact statement, narrative, timeline, and budget, your goal is to explore as many possibilities as you can, giving you more freedom to be creative in your thought process. At the same time divergent design strategies make visible the complexity of writing, they also enable us to be more inclusive, to think of diverse ways of doing and how best to reach diverse audiences. Such strategies help us see that designing isn't a simple, linear, or purely technical process, and they create spaces for us to have conversations that are diverse in nature. In other words, they can help address hidden assumptions and broaden participation.

4.3 Reframing Problems

As you might have sensed by now, this book has framed the designing of documents as problem-solving. Yet, divergent design principles allow us to take this a step further and reframe the actual problems we are working on to produce alternative solutions. In this reframing, we might ask, "What if?" or "Why not?" What if I had a small grant for my research project? Why not use funding to purchase *this* equipment rather than *that* equipment?

Over the years, many RCWS scholars have explored the concept of writing as nonlinear problem-solving, none more famous than Linda Flower and John R. Hayes. In their landmark 1981 article, "A Cognitive Process Theory of Writing," they argued that a writing problem is part of invention itself, that when we write, we define and redefine the problem many times over, thus creating multiple possibilities (p. 369). Their theory of writing connects these problem-solving inventive activities to our creativity. They write, "By placing emphasis on the inventive power of the writer, who is able to explore ideas, to develop, act on, test, and regenerate his or her own goals, we are putting an important part of creativity where it belongs-in the hands of the working, thinking writer" (p. 386). And that is also what divergent design principles do. The fact that they enable creative invention or ideation gives power to writers. Writers then have the ability not only to define the problem but also to reframe it, question it, and challenge it.

Reframing problems can be achieved in different ways, such as through role-playing, an action that can help us lead with empathy in our design choices. To use the grant proposal scenario example again, imagine yourself as a member of the panel or committee that will be assessing your grant proposal for the mid-level grant. Put yourself in their shoes. Do you want to offer the full amount to one project or split the total amount your organization can offer among many projects? They are going to invest time, money, and energy in reading, analyzing, and judging your proposal. What are their needs? How can you make their task easier? What have they approved in the past, and why? Take on the role of a panel member and work through your grant proposal.

Then, you could role-play again. This time, imagine you are working in your university's grant office. How might a research development specialist or a pre-award officer read your document differently than a representative of the award-granting organization? What do they need to get their job done, a job that will ultimately grant you your institution's permission to submit a final draft to the award-granting organization?

Finally, imagine one more role, that of a colleague who is in an entirely different field than yours. What might they need to understand your grant proposal? This role might highlight something that you or those involved in the grant can't see as an outsider would. This last role-playing suggestion could lead to an additional approach to reframing your problem. Sometimes, when we want to see a problem differently, it can be helpful to look beyond our inner circle or bubble to those who are unfamiliar with the problem or the context in which we are working and designing. In developing new perspectives of your problem (in this case, your problem is to write a successful grant for your research project), you might consider interviewing those in different fields and those beyond academia who work in a variety of industries, including those tangentially connected to or unrelated to your field. They may provide interesting takes on what your document could say about your research project.

4.4 Scenario: Writing a Job Advertisement

Imagine that you are leading a hiring committee, and your first task is to design a job ad for the position you wish to hire. You are given an example of a previous job ad your university used and are told to write something similar. You're asked to specify key areas of expertise in your field that your department lacks and to ensure the ad communicates that all qualified applicants should apply. Keeping the divergent design strategies in this chapter in mind, brainstorm multiple ways to reword the following ad so that it is specific and indicates that contingent faculty, international scholars, and candidates from historically underrepresented groups are both welcomed and encouraged to apply.

Job Ad:	ABC University seeks applicants for a full-time, tenure-track assistant or associate professor position. ABC University is an innovative liberal arts institution located in the metropolitan area of X City in the heart of the Midwest. Its core mission is to cultivate learning, integrity, and imagination, offering degrees in a wide range of subjects, from biology to business. It is a world-class research institute focused on creating future leaders of industries. At ABC University, we value a lively culture, collaboration among students and faculty, and academic excellence.

As a first step, frame this task as a complex problem; it includes multiple interdependent and unknown factors that you should consider. As you begin to brainstorm, consider what some of these might be and jot them down. Then, use a few GOOD divergent design principles to uncover possibilities that may be useful in this scenario. For instance, consider gathering input from people with diverse backgrounds and experiences to help you gain insight into the specialty or specialties you may need to include in the ad and how and where the ad might circulate.

4.5 Pushing Back Against Genre Conventions

As you learned earlier in this chapter, divergent design practices can help us broaden our perspectives, which can help us consider diverse ways of doing and seeing. This can lead us to push back against **genre conventions** that are exclusionary. RCWS scholars have long documented ways in which we should examine and subvert exclusionary genre conventions (see Bazerman, Bonini, and Figueiredo, 2009; Cano Jr., 2024; Wardle, 2009; Yancey, 2004). For example, Alexandria Lockett et al. (2021) provide a critical discussion of the grammar conventions of language representing race, ethnicity, and related content and delineate their decision-making processes on how and when they decided to align with conventions and resist them (pp. 4-7).

In addition to grammar conventions, scholars have also sought more equitable citation practices. Robert J. Connors (1999), a renowned scholar in RCWS, says, "The rhetoric of citation systems is fascinating because it has so silently undergirded the enterprise of Western intellectual activity. Though these systems constrain many of the ways we deal with each other and each other's work, they have largely gone unremarked" (p. 242). Building on Connors assertion, Candis Bond (2020) notes, "When students understand source selection and documentation as value-laden, they are positioned to better understand how these practices can contribute to social inequities within [...] disciplines, especially those related to gender" (para. 3). To illustrate one way in which we can create value-driven inclusive practices in our citation practices, we have included in this book the complete author names in the references lists, even though APA conventions call for only the first and, when available, middle initial.

Divergent design practices help us brainstorm alternative structures that give voice to those who may be marginalized otherwise. Faculty are familiar with quite a few genre conventions as they are often included in such documents as faculty manuals, such as procedures and policies. They also include instructions for preparing tenure dossiers or review portfolios, course syllabi or assignments, funding requests, and other design-based document features. Importantly, sometimes these are old, outdated, and exclusionary. It is up to us, then, to challenge these. Challenging conventions may mean using divergent thinking and imagining alternatives. The following chart offers examples of this kind of imagination. Creative reinterpretations of genres can promote inclusivity and better reflect contemporary communication practices.

TABLE 4.4 Genre Convention Alternatives Examples

Document Genre	*Conventions*	*Imagine...*
Syllabus	Headings, subheadings, schedules, assignment descriptions, learning objectives	Using comics, dialogue, or FAQs to inform your students what your class is about.
Thank you email	Salutation, signature, sentences, brief content	Creating a metaphor or analogy that demonstrates your gratitude.
Teaching philosophy	Subheadings, complete sentences, paragraphs, examples, practices, scholarly content	What a curated digital collection of your teaching materials might communicate rather than a one-page statement.

(*Continued*)

TABLE 4.4 (Continued)

Document Genre	*Conventions*	*Imagine...*
Job interview agenda materials	Title, headings, subheadings, schedule, interview questions, contact information	Writing questions for a job candidate that frame the interview as a conversation and identify themes your committee wants to cover.
Degree program description for prospective students	Paragraphs, concise language, prospective employment statistics, curriculum, timeline, financial resources	Creating a visual infographic of the program.
Department website	Pictures, headings, navigation menu, hyperlinks, mission statement, accomplishments, news/ events	Using student interviews of faculty, students, and alumni to tell the stories of your department, what it offers, and what it has accomplished.
Letter of recommendation for a colleague	Addresses, date, salutation, paragraphs, accomplishments, relationship, observations, and examples	Creating a video recommendation that includes student and colleague perspectives to illustrate the points you're making.

While divergent design enables you to creatively use invention to develop new unexpected ideas, it also helps you question the arrangement of ideas. If you take divergent design thinking, for instance, and apply it to the concept of information architecture introduced earlier in this book, you can find ways to push back against exclusionary genre conventions. To illustrate, documents like faculty manuals, assessment forms, tenure dossiers, grant applications, and so forth tell readers what they value based on their structure—how things are arranged, what comes first, second, and third, and what is emphasized by its placement on the page, in bold font. In fact, the structure is just as much of a storyteller as the content of the document itself. The structure tells readers what is valued and prioritized, as well as what is not valued at all. A faculty assessment form that begins with a lengthy description of accepted scholarship practices followed by a short section on service requirements may indicate to faculty that scholarship is the most important aspect of their job and service is recognized as less important. Faculty relying on or integrating service practices into their work, such as facilitating service learning or community-based experiential research, might feel their work is underappreciated because of the assessment form's structure. Traditionally, institutions often assess faculty on their teaching, research, administration, and service and often use these conventional names for labels (or categories) in their documents. But, as we have noted, for faculty whose work does not neatly fit into one of these categories, this could feel isolating or othering. In fact, they may feel that their work is invisible.

Indeed, effective information architecture should not only help users understand the content of documents but should also make users feel included. Imagining multiple ways of arranging, labeling, and building pathways for your readers is thus important. Truly, if you use GOOD divergent design principles as you reimagine as many different architectures as possible for your documents, you are better positioned to resist replicating a sole "correct" genre form. Different architectural structures can help us focus on marginalized voices, making sure our documents best serve all our audiences.

TABLE 4.5 Activity: Pushing Back on Genre Conventions

For this activity, work through the following steps to identify ways in which you can push back against genre conventions.

1. Choose a document genre (tenure application, CV, curriculum assessment form) and identify its purpose.
2. Gather ten examples (documents) from this genre.
3. Review them, making a list of the conventions, or features, they have in common.
4. Look beyond your field. Find out how other fields design documents in this genre. Collect examples and make notes about the conventions you see.
5. Imagine alternatives for your document. What can you do differently that would better suit your needs and the needs of your audiences? For example, should you choose a CV as your document genre, alternatives to a traditional printed version could include visual content illustrating grant funding or publication readership indexes or a portfolio webpage that uses categories as navigation labels and scroll-over pop-out boxes that contain content, including hyperlinks and multimodal materials.

Here are a few examples of alternatives for a CV to get you started:

- If your discipline values listing your credentials first on a CV, what happens when you list your teaching or your research first, or what happens when you list your grant funding later in your CV instead of upfront as is often the case in settings prioritizing award-based research?
- Can you challenge expectations through content organization and labels (as mentioned in this chapter)? For instance, what happens when teacher-researchers stop framing classes taught as "teaching" and instead move key course experience to research?
- What if you included dissertation advising in professional development, not in a section for teaching or service? Could this be an impactful way to bring light to the silenced work of dissertation advising?

Reordering sections, using hyperlinks, and layering information in different ways may help you design a document that disrupts "default" hierarchies. A course syllabus that contains a lot of policy text (which is often the case) may marginalize readers who are first-generation students and are unaccustomed to such jargon-heavy wording. While your university may restrict changing the policy sections of your syllabus, you can create a supplemental document that turns this content into a flowchart or an easy-to-read visual to help students feel welcomed into your class.

4.6 Uncovering Hidden Assumptions

In addition to pushing back against genre conventions, divergent practices can help us uncover hidden assumptions in institutional writing. For example, if you are a faculty member or a graduate student, your university has likely shared with you a faculty manual or student handbook. Each of these documents contains policies and procedures that faculty and students should abide by. However, these documents are often written by administrators who may have their own interests in mind that conflict with the interests of faculty or students. They may also assume their readers are fluent in institutional language and may not account for some audience members' circumstances. What if a faculty manual were written by contingent faculty? What if a student handbook were written by students? What would these look like? The answers to these questions might, for instance, highlight how different audiences use language differently as well as reveal how certain language privileges some while marginalizing others. They might also reveal what is a priority and how that priority can be represented through organization and structure.

If you were tasked to rewrite a faculty manual or student handbook, you might role-play as different users. If you were to rewrite a faculty manual's policy on parental leave, you might pretend you are a new contingent faculty member who is a single parent. If you were to rewrite a student handbook's policy on plagiarism, you might pretend you are an international student who comes from a country where plagiarism is thought of differently. This kind of role-playing helps to not only create an empathetic lens but also to identify the assumptions built into documents that might not be representative of all those who use them. Ultimately, recognizing these assumptions can enable ethical revisions for a more inclusive text.

Another divergent tactic to use when trying to uncover hidden assumptions would be to look for jargon or technical phrases and imagine replacing or substituting them with more inclusive language. If a faculty manual states that faculty "must engage in service to the community," you might consider what a wide range of faculty value, do, and need in that type of service experience. You could replace this phrase with a more specific, inclusive version that encourages and values a wide range of service contributions such as committee work, mentoring, leading student organizations, and so forth, across all faculty ranks and contract types. If, in a student handbook, a university stated that "students on academic probation have one year to demonstrate satisfactory academic progress to regain good standing," you might consider who the statement centers or values and what satisfactory academic progress means to a wide range of students. An alternative, perhaps more user-centered, statement might read: "Academic probation is a provisional status offering students a chance to refocus and recommit to their education. To help students regain good standing, the university offers a variety of support services to help students demonstrate satisfactory academic progress within one year of the start of probation status." Prioritizing the student's experience and needs and connecting the policy to extended resources, even vaguely, facilitates a more supportive and encouraging statement.

Yet another form of divergent thinking to uncover hidden assumptions can involve brainstorming what is missing from the manuals. We do make assumptions about what is not included in a document. For instance, a contingent faculty member who reads a faculty manual with no references to the word "contingent" in it might assume the manual does not support the work they do. Or they may feel less valued than full-time faculty. Finding ways that you could fill these gaps to better serve the diverse groups of people who will use this manual is particularly important when such a document pertains to labor practices and the ways in which that gets articulated.

TABLE 4.6 Activity: Trying Different Genres and Perspectives

For this activity, find a faculty handbook or student handbook and locate a policy statement, such as a leave of absence statement, plagiarism statement, statement on technology, etc. Rewrite this policy statement in three different genres (i.e., as a memo, infographic, narrative). Then, rewrite this policy from different user perspectives (i.e., as contingent faculty, department chair, staff member, student). Finally, reflect on the differences between the texts you create and the genre conventions you either adhered to or challenged when creating in different genres. What did you uncover?

4.7 How GenAI Can Be Leveraged with Divergent Design

As you work on finding all the available means for your documents by using GOOD divergent design principles, you might consider how GenAI can assist you in this endeavor. While you learned in Chapter 2 that GenAI cannot think like humans do, you can collaborate with it to imagine new possibilities for the documents you write. Going back to the example of the grant application from earlier in this chapter, you might, for instance, use GenAI to role-play. You could build a profile of a person who works as a research development specialist and insert that profile into your GenAI tool. You could then instruct the GenAI to act as this person as you share your grant proposal with the tool. As illustrated in this chapter's "What AI Has to Say" example, you could ask the GenAI to provide a range of feedback using different approaches or, if allowed by the grant-awarding organization, help you imagine different ways of writing the grant proposal based on the perspective of a research development specialist.

WHAT AI HAS TO SAY:

Researchers can test grant proposals with GenAI without uploading full documents by using targeted, section-by-section prompts.

Testing specific components: Instead of sharing the entire proposal, describe key elements in your prompt—like your research question, methodology, or significance statement—and ask GenAI to identify weaknesses, gaps, or unclear reasoning. For example: "Here's my proposed methodology: [brief description]. What questions would a skeptical reviewer ask?"

Simulating reviewer concerns: Describe your project's basic premise and ask GenAI to role-play as a program officer or panel reviewer from your discipline, generating likely questions or objections. This helps you anticipate concerns without revealing proprietary details.

Testing framing and positioning: Share just your project title and abstract, then ask GenAI how it would be perceived in your field, what competing approaches exist, or how to strengthen the positioning. This protects detailed methods while improving your pitch.

Checking logic and flow: Describe the structure of your argument (intro → gap → approach → expected outcomes) and ask GenAI to identify logical leaps or missing connections.

Budget justification review: Describe your budget categories and ask GenAI to role-play as a finance reviewer questioning whether items seem justified or appropriately categorized.

This approach maintains confidentiality while still leveraging GenAI's ability to simulate critical perspectives and identify potential weaknesses in your proposal's logic and presentation.

Code Credit: Anthropic, *Claude* (2026, January 3)

> Claude's output suggests traditional grant propposal structures and perhaps overlooks the diverse array of documents that educational professionals often create for award applications.

> Do these suggestions assume that all reviewers, administrators, or methodologists think alike? What stakeholders might we want to develop personas for if we're using Claude as a simulated responder? What kinds of specific questions could we ask to generate a range of feedback?

Example of an AI output generated with the prompt: "How can GenAI help an academic researcher test a grant proposal without requiring the researcher to upload the full proposal?" Code Credit: Anthropic, *Claude* (2026, January 3).

However, a few words of caution. When working with GenAI and research, protecting your work and aligning with institutional and organizational permissions remains a vital concern. Make sure you check with your university, any publications you intend to work with, and any organizations that may support the research to ensure you are not violating their standards. In the output example, note that Claude's output encourages working with small pieces of the proposal rather than the whole document. The output also recommends paraphrasing and describing content rather than uploading it. There are many approaches to working with GenAI that don't require uploading a complete document.

Also, as you learned in Chapter 2, output may appear to be close to the truth or sound correct but not be entirely accurate so you will need to roll up your sleeves and do the human work of checking it. This human work allows for reflection and, at this stage, that reflection should focus on what is possible no matter how far out it may be. Remember that when you engage in divergent design, you are trying to be creative and imaginative, to discover what you haven't thought of before. Whether in the end you use all the possibilities you generate doesn't matter. What matters is that you keep your options open.

4.8 Reflection

Returning to your own role in the writing process, using divergent design principles shines a light on what you can do differently to better communicate your messages as well as advocate for changes to the documents that are supposed to serve you. This is where reflection really comes in. Invention and arrangement require us to deeply think and reflect rhetorically about the ways documents are designed for us and by us.

As you use the GOOD divergent design principles you learned about in the beginning of this chapter, you might use the following questions as a reflection tool or checklist to help you consider if you have done enough to serve these two causes (to serve yourself and to serve others). This reflection is similar to the think, feel, say, and do reflection you used in Chapter 1 from Table 1.4: Problem-Solving Questions Using Lateral Thinking. Although you are expanding your design possibilities through divergent thinking in this chapter, you can also employ similar reflection techniques as you saw in Chapter 1. Table 4.7 offers a series of questions to help you get started.

TABLE 4.7 Reflecting on Divergent Design Using Lateral Thinking

Think	Feel
• How does using divergent design shift my way of thinking about my document? • Did I think about the impacts that my divergent designs will have on others?	• What feels uncomfortable, and how can this be useful? • Is there a more accessible, inclusive way of arranging my ideas?
Say	**Do**
• Did I ask someone outside my field to weigh in? • What does the order of my document's content say about what I value and will this exclude some of my readers?	• Have I brainstormed at least five alternatives to the design of my document? The structure? The content? The framing? • Did I consider the wildest, most unexpected without narrowing my options?

Answering these questions could lead you to even more possibilities, ones that once again challenge the kinds of documents you are creating and whether or not you have uncovered those hidden assumptions and/or exclusionary genre conventions that get in the way of making your voice heard.

When reflecting on divergent design principles, we also need to think of our own role as a designer. How does your positionality as a faculty member, a colleague, an instructor, and so on influence what you see as "professional?" After all, this book is about designing our professional documents, ones we use to perform our jobs, build our careers, make a name for ourselves, and help others. In this instance, it may be a good time to reflect on what we believe to be professional and how this thinking may center certain audiences over others. We often wear many hats in our careers and sometimes those can conflict. By reflecting on them and their relationship to how and what we design, we can position ourselves to make better design choices.

4.9 Chapter 4 Review

This chapter explains how we can use divergent design principles to create as many possibilities for our documents so that in the end, we are able to design more inclusive documents. These principles represent the rhetorical canons of invention and arrangement and utilize lateral thinking. Specifically, here are the key takeaways from this chapter:

- GOOD divergent design principles include generating abundance, originating novel approaches, optimizing creative thinking, and discovering the unexpected.
- Using GOOD divergent design principles means reframing our problems and questioning how the information architecture of our documents can better serve our audiences.
- Divergent design enables writers to challenge genre conventions and hidden assumptions and reflect on how they can design better documents as a result.
- GenAI can help us explore through several brainstorming activities, including role-playing, going beyond one's discipline, and thinking in opposites.

References

Anthropic. (2026, January 3). *Claude* (3.5 Sonnet) [Large Language Model]. https://claude.ai

Bazerman, Charles, Bonini, Adair, & Figueiredo, Débora. (2009). *Genre in a changing world*. The WAC Clearinghouse; University Press of Colorado.

Bond, Candis. (2020). Minding the (gender) gap: A rhetorical approach to teaching STEMM students about citations. *WLN: A Journal of Writing Center Scholarship*, *44*(7–8). 18–26.

Cano Jr., José Luis. (2024). Composition studies at the US-Mexico border. *College Composition and Communication*, *76*(2), 239–262.

Connors, Robert J. (1999). The rhetoric of citation systems, Part II: Competing epistemic values in citation. *Rhetoric Review*, *17*(2), 219–245.

Flower, Linda, & Hayes, John R. (1981). A cognitive process theory of writing. *College Composition and Communication*, *32*(4), 365–387.

Lockett, Alexandria L., Ruiz, Iris D., Sanchez, James Chase, & Carter, Christopher. (2021). *Race, rhetoric, and research methods*. The WAC Clearinghouse; University Press of Colorado.

Montague, Michel de. (1958). *Les Essais* (Donald M. Frame, Trans.). Standford University Press (original work published in 1580).

Wardle, Elizabeth. (2009). 'Mutt Genres' and the goal of FYC: Can we help students write the genres of the university? *College Composition and Communication*, *60*(4), 765–789.

Yancey, Kathleen Blake. (2004). Made not only in words: Composition in a new key. *College Composition and Communication*, *56*(2), 297–328.

5

CONVERGENT DESIGN

In the subtropical climate of south Florida, you will find banyan trees growing in urban neighborhoods and gardens. From these trees' trunks grow thick, horizontal branches. From these branches, grow aerial roots that shoot downward, planting themselves into the soil, acting as support for the branches above. A mature banyan tree is quite a sight to see with numerous branches and roots taking up large swaths of the landscape. In a sense this banyan tree represents divergent design as its many branches and roots symbolize the many possible ideas for our documents. As we move through divergent practices, we let our ideas grow in different directions, each time abstaining from pruning them down no matter how big or how twisted they get.

About 600 miles north of the urban cities of south Florida, away from the banyan trees, you will find the southernmost part of the Blue Ridge Mountains in northern Georgia. There, you will likely find a mountain stream or two. A mountain stream can serve as another metaphor, one for convergent design, the subject of this chapter. In the mountains, when snow melts, rain falls, and water trickles from springs, it moves down the mountain until it converges into a single stream. This stream, made of fragmented water from various places, takes shape and carves a distinct path down the mountain with a single destination in mind. This convergence is a narrowing; that is what we do when we move from divergent design to convergent design. We narrow our ideas into a single document that is strong enough to carry us to our destination. A stream is not a

DOI: 10.4324/9781003717232-8

stream without a unified purpose, a shape that is recognizable, and a flow that brings us somewhere specific. Not all the water from snowmelt, rain, or springs makes it into the stream—some gets absorbed in the soil, some evaporates. But, what is left gives the stream its shape and features, letting all those that happen upon it know that what they are looking at is indeed a stream, but one that is unique, unlike any other stream on the mountain. In other words, although all streams have certain features in common, there are no two that are exactly alike.

In a lot of ways, what happens in designing documents is much like what happens when a mountain stream is formed. Over time, our ideas trickle down into a recognizable design. We may use some common features of the genre we are writing in, but in the end, our document will be different, unique, from other documents, sometimes in subtle ways and at other times in bolder ways. That's because writing and designing documents is a rhetorical act. And, every rhetorical act is unique to the variables of its rhetorical situation. We as writers change, our audiences change, and the contexts in which we write change. In convergence, there is a narrowing, a shaping, and ideas do get lost along the way, but this is not a bad thing, but rather an integral part of the process for designing documents that work for us and others.

5.1 Sifting Through Divergent Ideas

When we use **convergent design**, we move away from exploring as many ideas as possible to choosing among these ideas in order to create a coherent text that best meets the needs of the rhetorical situation. Convergence is the point where the variables of the rhetorical situation come together effectively, from our narrowing down of ideas to the parameters we must work within (or against), to our awareness of our audience and self, to the technological and material resources to which we have access. Convergence is about focusing on what matters the most to us and our documents' users.

The narrowing down of ideas, however, is easier said than done, especially when we are working with many ideas or when we have a group of vastly different ideas. One way to approach this narrowing down is to rely on rhetorical thinking, linear thinking (at times), and the strategies in this book. Convergence is about focus. For instance, before we begin to prune our ideas and shape them into a document, we need to establish the elements of our rhetorical situation. From there, we can begin an initial filtering. Namely, we can start to determine what makes for viable ideas, the ones we will later develop into that final document. If you recall from this book's Introduction, to be successful in our documents, we, as writers/designers, need to understand ourselves, our purpose for communicating, our audiences, and our subject matter as part of our context for writing. This process of thinking about our situation helps us initially filter out some ideas that won't work. Think of this initial filtering as the water that doesn't make it to the stream. This step in the process involves:

- making sure that we are staying true to ourselves;
- acknowledging the needs of our audiences and creating a document that is inclusive;
- recognizing that the time and place for our document are right and that we have enough time and resources to be successful in the creation of it;
- ensuring the content we want to include is best represented by the type of text we want to write;
- identifying affordances and constraints (see Chapter 1) and how to work with them.

After doing this initial filtering, we can continue to narrow down our ideas keeping our rhetorical situation in mind. While divergent design's GOOD principles can help us expand our ideas, convergent design's **CORE principles** can help us narrow them. We use the word CORE to denote what we want to end up with when we finish narrowing: a focused document with a core idea.

TABLE 5.1 CORE Principles of Convergent Design

Principle	*What the Principle Means*	*Examples*
Categorize	To sort your ideas into groups to eliminate redundancies.	Organizing ideas by similarity, such as theme, tone, perspective, etc.
Order	To rank your ideas, giving more weight to those that help meet the needs of the rhetorical situation.	Prioritizing ideas by their feasibility, reach or impact, fit, accessibility, etc.
Refine	To prototype and test your ideas in order to revise them.	Creating drafts and testing them with different audiences using different protocols such as focus groups or think-out-loud user activities.
Enact	To prepare the final draft for circulation.	Finalizing the draft and delivering it to its intended audiences.

It may seem like the CORE principles are meant to be a process for elimination. They are, however, a process for judgment and decision-making. This is not a detached, impartial process. It requires attention to detail, to histories, to values, and to assumptions. It is at the same time rhetorical and reflective. Indeed, every choice you make should be based on how meaning gets made through your document and the people with whom you will share it.

5.1.1 Categorize

Using a filtering strategy to decide what ideas are similar can help reduce redundancies in your information. When we categorize the ideas we're working with, we often start with grouping, mapping, coding, or graphing ideas. When working with research data, you might assign a code to each data point based on a theme or category. Or, you might be more visual and opt for a graph that allows you to plot each data point in a representative quadrant. Some approaches to categorizing your information may lend themselves to the type of information you're using or to the purpose of your document. If you're on a team that's designing a new program, your information may be well-suited to chronological sorting. But, if you're on a team that's developing a white paper, you may be working with various types of information and choose to tag your data so that it's easier to track and organize.

It's equally important to consider who will be using the information and how they'll access it. Let's say, for example, that you are working on a book pitch that you will give to a publisher at an upcoming conference. Your goal is to create an effective pitch that will secure a book contract. After coming up with as many possible ways to begin this pitch, you use what you know of your rhetorical situation and begin to filter your ideas by grouping similar ideas into specific categories. If you find that you have a few ideas that are narrative-based, you might determine that you could begin your pitch with a story. If you group your ideas and realize you have a few interesting statistics, you might determine that another way to begin your pitch is with an interesting, jaw-dropping statistic related to your book's subject matter. Categorizing information by theme or genre (i.e., coding) can help you see trends in your data and correlate your information with audience needs or expectations. If you're pitching a publisher who works for a press that just published an ethnography, you might prioritize the story and use the statistics throughout the pitch. But, if the publisher's press is more inclined to publish quantitative research, you might choose to lead with your statistical information.

There are several ways in which you can group your ideas, and the following table presents a few of them that you might find helpful.

TABLE 5.2 Examples of How to Categorize

Coding Organize information by similarity (i.e., theme, genre, purpose) and identify each group by a representative word or phrase.	**Mapping** Organize information into segments or blocks based on purpose and/or audience needs. Rearrange blocks to find different logical information pathways.	**Sequencing** Organize information according to its position, purpose, or place in a process or event.	**Graphing** Organize information using visual representations such as charts or diagrams.
Approaches: tagging, indexing, color coding, labeling	**Approaches:** flowcharts, diagrams, concept or affinity mapping	**Approaches:** chains (cause-effect, problem-solution), scaffolding, ordering (chronological, spatial, importance)	**Approaches:** charting, matrix sorting, ranking

5.1.2 Order

The next step then is to assess the ideas within your categories and order them according to importance. In fact, you can rank and prioritize these ideas, giving special attention to your most promising ideas first. At this stage, you'll want to highlight the ones that will be most impactful and feasible. Think of this as a grading process where you weed out the ideas that are not of good quality based on your rhetorical situation. For instance, once you have your story ideas grouped together (i.e., coded) in a "story" category, you can go through them and determine which stories might work better for your audience, purpose, and the amount of time you will have with the editor to pitch your book. Not all stories can be told in the time you may have to tell them. Or, perhaps, you determine that your audience, the publisher's editor, has a special interest in something related to one of the stories on your list; you would deem this story valuable since it will help you build a connection with the editor.

Different approaches exist to assess ideas; depending on your document's or project's context, some may be more effective than others. It may be helpful, for instance, to develop a more qualitative or holistic rubric to help you prioritize your ideas, or you may need to pursue a thematic assessment to help you rank them. Alternatively, you may seek out more quantitative approaches, like the RICE method (McBride, 2018) or the Kano Model (Olsen-Landis, 2017).

The **RICE method** includes assessing an idea for its reach, impact, confidence, and effort and can be helpful in determining the cost-benefits of your ideas. This method quantifies an idea using the formula (reach*impact*confidence)/effort; however, it can be modified to meet your context as needed. At its most basic model, RICE requires determining the reach of each idea or identifying how many people in your audience may be affected by the idea in a specific timeframe (this becomes your first number). Then, you assess the idea for its potential impact, which includes considering the ways in which that impact may manifest for your audience and how the idea affects the information you are communicating. Score the idea on a rating scale from 3 (massive impact) to .5 (low impact). The third step is then to assess your confidence in the previous two scores. Depending on the level of confidence you have that the previous two numbers are accurate and achievable, you'll rate confidence as 100 (high), 80 (moderate), or 50 (low). Finally, you will determine the time it takes to bring the idea to completion. This can be measured using any standard of time, but months is the most common.

TABLE 5.3 Activity: Using the RICE Method to Order Your Ideas

For this activity, brainstorm ideas for a new document and then categorize those ideas using one of the suggestions in this chapter. Next, use the RICE method to assess these ideas and order them according to their scores. To help you get started, here is an example of what that might look like. Let's say that you are applying for jobs and that you need to create a CV to do so. You brainstorm ideas for what this CV will look like, and one of those ideas is to create a digital gallery CV. Another is to create a traditional text-based CV. Here is how you could use the RICE method to determine if the digital gallery CV would be a good idea.

- Reach: You anticipate you'll apply to ten jobs and estimate about three people per application review committee. Your reach number is 30.
- Impact: You anticipate that the unique delivery method of this information will resonate with reviewers and become a talking point in committee discussions, but you are aware that this document structure could be viewed as confusing, so you go with a conservative rating of 1.
- Confidence: You know you may have underestimated your audience, but it's a logical audience size for the first round of application reviews, and there's a chance the impact could be closer to a "2" or "3," but you wanted to err on the side of caution. You rate your confidence score at 80.
- Effort: You think it will take you two weeks to design and storyboard, three weeks to code and compile, and one week to revise and refine (6 weeks total). A score of "2" indicates two months of work.

Your formula is (30*1*80)/2, and your RICE score is 1200. Now, you could compare this to how your remaining idea (a traditional text-based CV) scores and rank both your ideas with the highest score receiving the highest priority.

Unlike the RICE method, the **Kano model** focuses on a needs-based assessment and works best when you have access to your audience. This model focuses on asking users to identify basic performance, attractor, indifferent, and reverse needs associated with the idea or product in question. The Kano model asks audiences (users) to assess the features that are required for the product to function (basic performance), unexpected features that enhance the use (attractors), features that don't impact the user experience (indifferent features), and elements that diminish the user experience (reverse needs).

Returning to the example in Table 5.3, if we are using the Kano model to assess the quality of our digital gallery CV, we would provide our audience with a storyboard of the gallery site and ask them to rate elements in each category using Likert scales for satisfaction and performance, or we might simply offer guided opportunities for users to provide written or spoken feedback. Our assessment would include common elements expected in a CV, such as professional experience, research, and service. We might ask our users to identify their satisfaction with the clarity of information provided or the number of examples included in the digital gallery. If we are testing the quality of the user experience with our digital gallery, we would also include features required of a digital site, such as site mapping and navigation. Additionally, we would need to ask our audience to provide feedback on the "add-on" features—elements that aren't necessary but are included in our site design to enhance the user experience—such as popovers added to further clarify content in the research section of our gallery or hyperlinks added to direct viewers to sites where community or institutional service is represented.

After collecting the feedback, we would analyze the data and plot responses to help determine where we should place our efforts in the next step of convergence, refinement. Using the Kano model, we would prioritize the necessities of the design, ensure we have attractors, and aim to eliminate the reverse-needs elements in our gallery prototype. If, for example, users responded positively to the clarity of how we've represented research and noted that the popovers created a cluttered feeling, we would prioritize refining the popovers to mitigate the negative experience, or we might consider omitting them altogether. While quantifiable outcomes can easily be determined with this model, understanding design priorities often requires synthesizing information in ways that align it more directly with a mixed approach.

Whether you're using a quantitative, qualitative, or mixed approach to your assessment, it's important to remember that all assessment frameworks have strengths and weaknesses. The RICE method, for example, quantifies assumptions. You're making educated, informed guesses as to the size of your audience and the impact of your idea, so the numbers are somewhat arbitrary. But, the experience of ranking these aspects may reveal considerations you hadn't yet identified.

5.1.3 Refine

After you have initially assessed and ordered your ideas, it is now time to prototype them and test whether you really do indeed have the best ideas in your document's design. This strategy involves not only sketching, prototyping, and testing but also refining and improving the ideas so that you can optimize your design. Importantly, assessment is as integral to refining your design as it is to ordering your ideas. For instance, using the example from earlier about developing a book pitch to be delivered to an editor at a conference, you could draft your pitch's opening lines and then share them with a few of your colleagues. Based on the feedback you receive, you can then refine and improve this draft.

As you refine your idea, consider drafting more than one version so that you and others can compare them. Treat each draft as data since each will help you determine which ideas resonate and which fall flat. Consider testing your ideas with different audiences to get diverse feedback. Finally, reflect on what the data tell you. It may reveal hidden assumptions or reveal a perspective you hadn't considered, giving you a new direction to follow. Refining is just as much about improving ideas and drafts as it is about invention.

Here are some suggestions for how you can test your ideas. These are testing strategies that can pair well with information in the next chapter on usability and accessibility testing.

TABLE 5.4 Different Methods for Testing Ideas

Method	*Use*	*Considerations*
Reverse outline	This works best for print-based documents.	Before you draft, you may use an outline. But, consider outlining your draft once it is complete to see what you actually wrote and compare this to your rhetorical situation, making sure that it lines up with your audience's needs and your intended purpose.
Usability walkthrough	This works best for documents that include instructions, require audiences to move about (like what happens on a website), and have nonlinear pathways.	Ask your audience to follow your instructions, move about to find particular information or parts, and make note of when your audience gets lost, stuck, or misinterprets information.

(*Continued*)

TABLE 5.4 (Continued)

Method	*Use*	*Considerations*
Reflective journaling	Works best when you are drafting complex documents and will need multiple rounds of testing.	Ask your audience to work with your document several times. After each time, question your audience and make reflective notes about their feedback.
This or that	This works best when you can draft multiple versions.	Give your readers two versions (whether two openings, two titles, two closings) and ask your audience which one they find more effective.
Role-play the audience	This works best when you do not have access to audiences.	Assume the role of your intended audience and consider how they would approach your document, what questions they might ask, how they might use it, and in what order.

5.1.4 Enact

Finally, you will produce your final polished draft for delivery. During this time, you will edit and proofread because at this point, you won't have big changes to make, but rather small ones. For example, once you choose the story you will tell at the beginning of the book pitch, you will spend time working on word choice, punctuation, and syntax. It is a time to think about the delivery, how the document will appear, circulate, and perform. In what form will it be delivered (i.e., PDF file, printed, spoken), and what preparations must be made to make this work?

In addition, polishing a draft doesn't just mean making sure you have grammatically correct sentences. It is actually more than this. It includes thinking rhetorically; for instance, making sure the tone matches the document's purpose and is appropriate for the audience.

Most importantly, this is where you finalize the bridge between divergence and convergence and the final time you can step back and reflect on your document—more on reflection later in this chapter. This is your chance to own your work, to determine if this is what best represents you as a professional in your discipline. Your documents reflect your credibility.

Ensuring a document is ready for distribution and circulation should be less about perfecting surface-level correctness based on biased Western standards (as the "What AI Has to Say" example implies) and more about

WHAT AI HAS TO SAY:

Polish Language and Style
This is the surface-level refinement that affects readability and professionalism.
Strategies:

- Read aloud to check rhythm, flow, and sentence variety.
- Replace heavy nominalizations with verbs ("conduct an analysis of" > "analyze").
- Eliminate redundancies ("each and every," "past history," "final outcome").
- Adjust transitions for coherence ("however," "for example," "in addition").
- Tighten modifiers and pronouns to clarify reference ("this" > "this study," "this idea").
- Ensure parallel structure in lists and bullet points.

Prompt:
"Can I read this paragraph aloud without tripping? If not, what sentence rhythm needs attention?"

> This assumes a universal style and a somewhat singular rhetorical situation. How do we know what a polished language or style looks like? Who determines this standard? For example, we might need to use nominalizations for readability. Or, perhaps our audience or our subject doesn't need us to repeatedly specify modifiers.

Enhance Visual and Spatial Design
Polishing includes the delivery of your design — how readers encounter it visually.
Strategies:

- Apply consistent heading hierarchy (size, weight, and spacing).
- Ensure margins, alignment, and white space guide the eye naturally.
- Use typographic emphasis (bold, italics, bullet points) sparingly and purposefully.
- Check accessibility: contrast, readable fonts, alternative text for visuals.
- For multimodal pieces (slides, PDFs, web pages), ensure layout complements tone and content.

Prompt:
"Where does my reader's eye go first, and is that where I want it to go?"

> This privileges a linear design with a clear hierarchy (or the need for one). These instructions offer little to no guidance for visual elements or an overall design that resists dominant genre conventions or seeks to adapt to users' differences.

Check Coherence and Flow
This is about logic, pacing, and transitions—moving from micro-edits to global cohesion.
Strategies:

- Create a reverse outline: Write one sentence per paragraph summarizing its function.
- Look for repetition or drift: Does every paragraph serve a purpose?
- Check transitions between sections: Do ideas connect clearly?
- Read the introduction and conclusion back-to-back: Do they frame the same argument or story arc?
- Test paragraph openings: Are your topic sentences clear and engaging?

Prompt:
"Could a reader skim my first sentences and understand the overall structure?"

Code Credit: OpenAI, *ChatGPT* (2025, November 18)

> As we've seen with the examples in the previous chapters, this output neglects cultural difference. How might we prompt our AI to provide more inclusive suggestions? What could we add here to ensure accurate representation of our document's user?

Example of an AI output generated with the prompt: "Can you give me more suggestions for how to polish a draft?" Code Credit: OpenAI, *ChatGPT* (2025, November 18).

meeting the demands of the rhetorical situation, one that accounts for how, when, where, and with whom the document will be distributed and circulated. In other words, how it will live and the relationships it will have with its intended audience. A design is ready for distribution and circulation when it can build these relationships and align itself with the people who use it. To give some examples of how one may approach responsible enactment, you might answer a question such as, "How does my language harm people?" rather than a question such as, "Is that word spelled correctly?" Instead of focusing on reducing wordy sentences and making them more concise, you might focus on the history of the words you use and what they can mean to different people. Are they dangerous? What would be the repercussions of using them? Rather than eliminate uses of "I" or "me" from your writing, you might consider how your intended audience may welcome such a centered voice as opposed to a passive, distant one. Do they come from a place where knowledge is shared in personal, informal ways? The readiness of your document's design makes a significant difference for its audience. We can think of it as the difference between an open door and one that is closed. A document that is ready has an open door. One we might not even notice because we walk through it with ease. But a closed door is visible; it requires effort to access what's on the other side.

Earlier in this section you read that convergence is about focus. At the same time, it is also about responsibility. That responsibility includes ethical decision-making. We are not just eliminating or reducing; we are making judgments based on how people will interpret and use our documents. We must consciously address how the meaning that will result from our documents will shape current and future knowledge in positive and negative ways. Narrowing down often controls whose voices are heard and whose are not. It is up to us to make design decisions that don't intentionally or unintentionally marginalize people. To be an inclusive designer means to not lose sight of this in convergence.

5.2 Using GenAI and CORE Convergent Design Principles

GenAI can help demonstrate convergence's CORE principles in action. For example, let's say you have been tapped to create a page on your department's website to showcase a new program your department started this past year. After you brainstorm as many possibilities for the design and content of the page, you are ready to employ convergent design strategies with the help of GenAI.

To aid with categorizing your ideas, you first provide GenAI with a list of all the possible ideas you developed and ask it to put like or similar ideas into labeled categories, helping you to narrow your list down by eliminating redundancies. In other words, GenAI could code your ideas, assigning them to a particular group.

Next, you share information about your rhetorical situation with your GenAI, such as your purpose and audience for the page, and ask it to order the ideas (that are now organized into categories) by how feasible and impactful they will be. You give the GenAI a ranking system, assigning (1) as the most feasible and impactful, (2) as somewhat feasible and impactful, and (3) as the least feasible and impactful. To put it differently, the GenAI will help you rank your ideas from most likely to succeed to least likely to succeed.

Once this happens, you can move on to drafting a few different versions of the page, starting with the ideas the GenAI ranked as 1. After which, you can share these drafts once again with your GenAI and prompt it for feedback. For instance, you might ask it to test whether you have all the necessary information about the new program or whether users who land on the page can navigate it successfully. You could even go so far as to give the GenAI a task to complete. For example, on the page, if you included steps for registering for the department's program for students who are interested in participating, you could prompt the GenAI to summarize these steps. You could use this summary to determine if your steps make sense. It may show you that a step is missing or that a step is unclear. In any case, this could help you revise.

Finally, you can use GenAI to help you polish and produce your final draft, making sure that it is ready to deliver to your intended audience. You could ask the GenAI to determine if the language is clear and concise, appropriate for your intended audience, and what might you do differently with the language to account for your rhetorical situation.

Keep in mind that GenAI's output will likely be flat or prescriptive, like the example provided at the end of Section 5.1.4 Enact. In some instances, this may be helpful. For example, if you aren't used to refining your content, the prescriptive approach offered in this AI box will likely be helpful. However, if you've developed a practice of revising and refining your writing, this guide may be too limiting to be useful. You'll want to critically consider when and how to integrate GenAI into your convergence process.

Working with GenAI using convergent practices does not relieve you, as the designer, of decision-making. As you have learned in this book, working with AI technologies requires human work. Remain vigilant in your use of GenAI to narrow down your ideas. The decision-making you will do is not a matter of determining whether the output is usable. Rather, part of your work in the human–AI relationship is determining whether the output aligns with your values and engages your audiences in ethical, equitable, and inclusive ways. Remember, AI is not the final authority on any subject. It is a tool that we can use cautiously and carefully to think through our ideas.

TABLE 5.5 Activity: Using GenAI Prompts for CORE Convergent Design

There are three steps for this activity. The first step is to develop prompts for GenAI, the second is to reflect on the outputs generated by them, and the third is to revise the prompts to use them again. Before you begin, choose a document you are currently working on and generate as many possibilities or ideas for it. Then, perform the following steps:

Step 1: Keeping the CORE principles (categorize, order, refine, enact) in mind, develop prompts you can input into GenAI to help you with the narrowing of your ideas. For instance, using the example in Section 5.2, if you were developing a page to showcase a new department program, you might start with the following prompt to help you group your initial ideas.

Prompt 1: I am currently planning a webpage to explain a new program at my university. Here is a list of items that I would like to include on the webpage. Please help me group these items into categories.

Step 2: Reflect on the generated output. Observe how the GenAI categorized the items on your list. What items on your list did it combine? What categories did it generate, and will these be useful? You might, for example, find that the names of the categories could serve as section headers on the webpage. For example, perhaps on your list of items for the new program's webpage, you listed student demographics (current enrollment), student stories about the program (what they like about it), and examples of student work created in the program. Perhaps, the output combined these into a category called "Student Experience." This category might make for a helpful subheading on your webpage.

In addition, you might find that the GenAI output asked you for further clarification. For instance, perhaps it asks you to offer suggestions for category labels to help it understand what might fit together.

Step 3: Finally, revise your prompt and try it again. This may help you think differently about your ideas. For instance, if you don't like the initial categories or groups your GenAI developed, try a more focused prompt. Using the same example, perhaps a different prompt about the webpage might look like this:

Prompt 2: I am currently planning a webpage to explain a new program at my university in order to attract more students. Here is a list of items that I would like to include on the webpage. Please help me group these items into categories that center students first.

This prompt may generate a new voice for your ideas, such as one that speaks directly to students using categories like "Where this program can take you" and "How to sign up." Reflect on the outputs from each of your prompts until you find ones that work for you. Remember, working with AI means doing human work; that is, you must engage in active thinking and reflecting when using AI.

5.3 Inclusive Design

Throughout this book, you have learned strategies for pushing back on exclusionary genre conventions and have been encouraged to think critically about exclusionary writing practices. These strategies have asked you to think about your own needs as well as to empathize with others and their needs. While it may seem like these strategies are more applicable with the creativity prioritized with lateral thinking or the vast possibilities generated through divergent design, inclusive strategies are equally applicable when using convergent design and with linear thinking. Advocating for changes through strategic convergent design decisions, as previously mentioned, should be a priority so that your documents can be inclusive of all stakeholders, including yourself.

Inclusive design means to design a document deliberately so that it anticipates and assists a range of users. Such a design focuses on fairness, user-friendliness, and flexibility, recognizing that users vary in identity, language, ability, access, and context. It is about designing a text that has numerous points of participation. When narrowing your ideas down through convergent design, you can design for inclusiveness and find clever ways to push boundaries. Convergence doesn't mean that you have to default to traditional genre expectations.

To illustrate, let's say you are in charge of a hiring committee, and your first task is to write a job advertisement for the position your committee is tasked to hire. Your committee gathers up previous job advertisements from your university as well as others, and you observe that most begin with a statement boasting about the prestige of the hiring institution, such as "The institution is a nationally ranked R1…." The message this sends implies what they can offer job candidates: time and resources to support research.

However, your committee feels this approach is not inclusive and decides to brainstorm other ways to begin a job ad. Committee members discuss the advertisements that begin with descriptions of campus, department mission statements, and summaries of the job expectations. After which, your committee members get to work narrowing these ideas down into a draft that more closely reflects the department's priority, which is creating an inclusive educational environment. To do this narrowing, the committee first groups the ideas into three categories that speak to inclusivity: mentoring, community, and engagement. From there, your committee orders them, ranking the ones that will have the biggest impact first. Next, your committee creates two versions of the opening lines of the ad, which you then share with your colleagues who are not on the committee and your department chair for their feedback. Using their feedback, your committee refines and finalizes a draft that better represents your department's ideals.

In fact, in the end, your committee's advertisement doesn't begin with a statement about the university's prestige like many of the others your committee looked at, but rather, it begins with a statement about its commitment to fostering an engaging community of learners.

Such an example demonstrates that when it comes to convergent design and linear thinking, your document does not have to follow a traditional format or replicate a trend. Convergent design doesn't have to lead to the same old documents. Instead, it is possible to deliberately choose and refine your divergent alternatives to create a nontraditional document that successfully serves your intended audiences while at the same time best represents you. RCWS scholarship has long noted that standard document genre features and templates have privileged some bodies while excluding others. Although writing about Web 2.0 design practices, or lack thereof, much of what Kristin L. Arola argued in 2010 resonates with what we are experiencing today. Templates, as she pointed out, take away our agency as writers/designers, leaving us with "little control over a large part of our representation" (p. 7).

When it comes to inclusive design, RCWS scholarship that links design to social justice provides a framework for reflection. Some scholars, such as Sasha Costanza-Chock (2020), prefer to call it **design justice**. As she writes, "Design justice asks whether the affordances of a designed object or system disproportionally reduce opportunities for already oppressed groups of people while enhancing the life opportunities of dominant groups, independently of whether designers intend this outcome" (p. 41). Her work on social justice points to the inequalities produced across different technologies, highlighting how design that is made for the majority, often already privileged people, truly marginalizes underrepresented people. What she suggests we do instead is to "destabilize the underlying assumption that what is best for the majority of users is best for all users" (p. 58). Designing for as many people as possible (i.e., universal design) should not be confused with designing for the majority (i.e., hegemonic design). Designing for as many people as possible accounts for diverse bodies.

Likewise, in advocating for iterative design as a social justice practice, Liz Lane and Kristen R. Moore (2023) show us how recursive and reflective designing can lead us to resist harmful norms and push back against exclusionary practices. They argue that "Each opportunity to design a solution is an opportunity to combat injustice within a communicative space. Just as persuasion is a complex aim for a rhetor to navigate, design is a delicate process to assuring justice and avoidance of harm" (p. 31). Good design, they go on to say, forces us to slow down and think through the problems we face but also allows for marginalized voices to be heard.

What this book posits, and what RCWS scholars suggest, is that we do not need to nor should we always default to a de facto template or standard form. They tend to be exclusionary, especially when representing marginalized voices. As Arola writes, when we stop actively participating in design production, we end up with "less critical consciousness not only about the meaning design conveys but also the ways in which that meaning is enmeshed with the world around us" (pp. 7-8). This is indeed worrisome, which is why we should not fear moving beyond standard forms and templates. As Costanza-Chock points out, "Discriminatory design often operates through standardization" (p. 43). Moving beyond standard forms or templates gives us the agency we need to be creative and inclusive.

Keeping this in mind, we can use the following to move beyond the standard when designing for inclusivity. This is not an all-encompassing list, however, and working to identify other ways to design inclusive documents should become part of your creative practice.

- Transparency—making sure your ideas are stated clearly and without insider jargon that may exclude some users.
- Empathy—making sure your ideas and design not only account for but also value difference instead of assuming sameness.
- Representation—making sure your ideas and design do not exclude any perspectives and voices. Depictions should be authentic and consider all, not some.
- Equity—making sure all readers/users get what they need in order to meaningfully access and engage with your document. This includes users with physical difference, literacy difference, and cultural difference.

Employing these strategies should happen not just in your wording, but across all the modes you are using in your documents (whether they are linguistic, oral, spatial, or visual modes). Choosing color and contrast as well as font sizes, for instance, are rhetorical choices that indicate to users that you care about their diverse abilities and needs.

Although Chapter 6 discusses the importance of feedback and assessment, it is worth noting here that inclusive design is not about a checklist that helps us ensure we have diverse features in our designs. It is an iterative drafting practice that must include others. In other words, we must examine together what makes our designs comprehensive. Without even realizing it, our designs might be exclusionary because we fail to share them, invite conversations about them, welcome interrogations of them, and listen to interpretations of them.

By now, you may have noticed that testing and refining are an integral part of convergent design. Testing, especially when you share your documents with diverse readers gives you the opportunity to recognize prejudices and barriers before you disseminate your final draft.

TABLE 5.6 Activity: Equity in Design

For this activity, find a recent document you created for your department, college, professional organization, or grant funding institution. Next, discover whether you have used transparency, empathy, representation, and equity by answering the following questions or any additional questions you create when thinking about the meaning of these terms. Then, make plans for purposeful revisions.

Inclusive practices		Planned revisions
Transparency	What terms, words, or phrases need to be defined or written in plain language? Are there any unclear expectations for any of my readers?	
Empathy	Have I considered the differences my readers/users might have and treated these as assets or difficulties? Does my document account for the emotional experiences of my audiences? Is the tone I use inviting or authoritative?	
Representation	Have I considered who might be privileged or misrepresented by my document? Whose voices are reflected in this document and whose are not?	
Equity	Will everyone who reads/uses my document be able to engage with it in a meaningful way? Have I built in, whether through wording or through other modes like visuals, multiple pathways for understanding?	

Remember that testing should not be the only time you actively design for inclusivity. Inclusive design starts at the beginning of the process and remains a valued goal throughout your project's development.

5.4 Identifying Constraints

In convergent design, you will still have constraints to work within. Constraints are any conditions, borders, or parameters that determine what is and is not possible and can act as additional filters to help you narrow down your ideas as long as they do not interfere with inclusion. Returning to the hiring committee example in the previous section, your committee's job advertisement will probably be restricted to a word or character limit because of the platforms you will use to post the advertisement and distribute it to possible candidates. This constraint informs the committee's choices for content, language, tone, and organization. There may be information in the committee's original draft that is too complex or too wordy, and a different organizational structure may allow more concise descriptions of the job expectations or community.

Another way to look at constraints is to think of them as possibilities rather than limitations. As possibilities, constraints can define the space for your design, inform your timeline and scope, and help you frame your audience. Framed this way, constraints become another way for you to be productive in creating a successful document.

As you work to design your documents, it is important to recognize that constraints come in different forms. To help you identify those with which you are working, consider the following types of constraints and how you might best use them to your advantage:

- Institutional—your department, college, and/or university's policies, standard forms, or templates.
- Material—the document size, word count and space, color and typography, and substance (physical and/or digital).
- Temporal—production deadlines, relevancy, and duration of user access.
- Spatial—location of the design, its delivery and distribution, and its users' access; limitations may also occur within the document.
- Users—your audiences' expectations, accessibility needs, preferences, and knowledge.
- Financial—the cost to produce, access, or use a document.
- Ethical—the values and priorities of the designer, user, and/or representative organizations.
- Technological—the technologies involved in creating, accessing, or using the document. Technological literacies, such as how to create or navigate an editable PDF, are also a part of this constraint.
- Genre—the standard design elements for a particular type of document and the expectations a reader has for that document.

When facing limited options, writers/designers have to make careful, resourceful decisions to find creative paths forward. That isn't to say that all limitations can be fixed or are unmovable, but it is up to us to challenge and negotiate when possible.

5.5 Scenario: Promoting an Event

For this scenario, imagine that your dean has asked you to develop a flyer for an upcoming college-wide research symposium that will take place in a month and a half from now. The flyer will be distributed in two weeks via email to all faculty to encourage their participation in the event. After you have developed a list of all possible ideas for the flyer, you begin to narrow this list down by identifying the constraints of your rhetorical situation.

TABLE 5.7 Activity: Identifying Constraints and Responding

Using the scenario in Section 5.5, make a list of constraints that you may encounter when designing a flyer for the symposium and what creative steps you could take to work with or against them. Refer to the list of constraints provided in Section 5.4 Identifying Constraints. Your list might include institutional constraints that identify limitations and possibilities established by your university and by your department, and response(s) to these constraints:
Institutional constraints—university: colors, font, and logo must align with university brand expectations
Response to these constraints: check the university brand guide and ensure flyer meets these expectations.
Institutional constraints—department: language must be inclusive and equitable
Response to these constraints: identify faculty readers who can review flyer content for exclusionary language and design elements and offer feedback
The list of constraints provided in Section 5.4 is not exhaustive. After working through the categories listed, consider additional constraints you may be working with in this scenario.

5.6 Information Architecture and Convergence

Yet another way to help with design convergence is to use information architecture. As you learned in Chapter 3, information architecture centers the user experience by structuring information in ways that acknowledge user logic. Put simply, it provides coherence and reduces the amount of work users must do to find and understand information. As mentioned, information architecture utilizes organization, labeling, navigation, and search capabilities and values flexibility, clarity, integration, and scalability. This framework is beneficial for optimizing design and producing documents as its categories can guide you in developing assessment criteria for your ideas and your prototypes. It can also assist you in determining optimal approaches to distribution and circulation. In this chapter, you have learned quite a bit about labeling through the process of categorizing (the "C" in CORE) and organizing through order (the "O" in CORE), but all information architecture concepts play a part in convergence. As a case in point, members of your audience need to be able to navigate and search your documents, too. Building a design that makes finding information easy for your audiences means you will have to be strategic in your choices.

TABLE 5.8 Activity: Test Navigation of Content in a Design

For this activity, locate your university or college website's home page and test how you navigate it using the following prompts. Then, reflect on your experiences.

First, choose a major or minor that your college or department offers. Then, from the homepage, without using a search function, navigate to the area on your college or department's website (or webpage) that instructs current students about the coursework and program requirements they must complete in order to graduate with this major or minor.

- What helps you navigate to or locate this information? For example, does your department's website use labels? Hyperlinks? Bold font?
- What doesn't help you navigate or locate this information? In other words, what is missing, or what gets in the way of you finding the information?

Next, from your university or college website's homepage and without using a search function, navigate to or locate information about your department's faculty, such as their contact information.

- What helps you navigate to or locate this information? For example, does your department's website use labels? Hyperlinks? Bold font?
- What doesn't help you navigate or locate this information? In other words, what is missing, or what gets in the way of you finding the information?

Finally, from your university or college website's homepage and without using a search function, navigate to or locate information about scholarships potential students could apply for if they want to enroll in one of your department's programs.

- What helps you navigate to or locate this information? For example, does your department's website use labels? Hyperlinks? Bold font?
- What doesn't help you navigate or locate this information? In other words, what is missing, or what gets in the way of you finding the information?

5.7 Reflection

Much like you did in the previous chapter when employing divergent design strategies, you will again want to reflect, this time as you employ convergent design strategies. To help you with this reflection, try using the following list of questions:

TABLE 5.9 Reflecting on Convergent Design Using Lateral Thinking

Think	Feel
• How does using convergent design shift my way of thinking about my document? • Did I think about the impacts that my convergent designs will have on others?	• What feels uncomfortable, and how can this be useful? • Is there a more accessible, inclusive way of arranging my ideas given the constraints I encounter? • Who might find my document confusing or unwelcoming?
Say	**Do**
• What does my document say about what I value? • What does my document say about my users' identities, time, or resources?	• Did I test different versions of my draft with different audiences? • How can I design my document to better empower my users?

The reflection that you do at this stage should enable you to critically think about the assumptions you made in your document's design and give you a path forward for refining your draft to better include all users.

Although we present convergent design in the penultimate chapter of this book, convergent design practices are not an exclusive final stage for document design. Like reflection, convergent design can occur at any point in your design process. These practices can often serve as a beginning. Notably, it is through these practices that you begin to hold your design accountable in the real world. It is here that you often start making ethical judgments that have real consequences for your users. Instead of flattening your work, in a sense, convergence opens it up to existence in a culture, an environment, a system. We choose how our documents can and should live and move through the world.

5.8 Chapter 5 Review

This chapter explains convergent design strategies that help writers and designers move from divergent design practices to crafting final drafts that best serve their users. This move necessitates that you narrow down your ideas to those that are most impactful, practical, and feasible given your rhetorical situation. Specifically, in this chapter, you learned about:

- convergent design's CORE principles, a framework for turning abundance into clarity and coherence, which includes categorizing, ordering, refining, and enacting;

- narrowing as a reflective activity because it requires active critical thinking to ensure a document's usability;
- creatively strategizing how to work with and against both exclusionary genre conventions and constraints;
- using information architecture to help test ideas and ensure your documents are accessible to all users.

References

Arola, Kristin L. (2010). The design of web 2.0: The rise of the template, the fall of design. *Computers and Composition*, *27*(1), 4–14.

Costanza-Chock, Sasha (2020). *Design justice: Community-led practices to build the worlds we need.* The MIT Press.

Lane, Liz, & Moore, Kristen R. (2023). The invisible work of iterative design in addressing design injustices. *Technical Communication & Social Justice*, *1*(2), 28–48.

McBride, Sean (2018, January 5). *RICE: Simple prioritization for product managers.* Intercom. https://www.intercom.com/blog/rice-simple-prioritization-for-product-managers

Olsen-Landis, Cary-Anne. (2017, March 23). *Kano model—Ways to use it and NOT use it.* Medium. https://medium.com/design-ibm/kano-model-ways-to-use-it-and-not-use-it-1d205a9cf808

OpenAI. (2025, November 18). *ChatGPT* (GPT-5) [Large Language Model]. https://chatgpt.com

6

TRANSFORMATIVE SPACES

When Jasper, a new assistant professor, designed a syllabus for his history course, he wanted it to look "professional" and "inviting." Using both divergent and convergent practices, he first came up with several different possibilities for the design and then narrowed those down into one document. In the end, he included color-coded sections, text in boxes, a sleek font, and decorative icons related to the course's assigned readings and assignments.

However, during week four of the semester, a student approached him after class and indicated that the syllabus was hard to read with a screen reader. In fact, the student said her screen reader could not navigate the headings at all. That is when Jasper realized that while his syllabus may have looked good, it was not accessible and that he had failed to meet the needs of his users. Indeed, it wasn't just a case of failing to run his document through an accessibility checker—which he had not. It was a matter of failing to recognize his own assumptions. He had assumed, incorrectly, that everyone who received his document would be able to use it and would do so in the same way.

The consequences for his failed design were many. It was now apparent that his student didn't feel welcome in his class, and she was struggling. Not to mention, because of his design choices, she had been working harder than the other students in the class for the past four weeks, which likely took away from other things in her life and produced unnecessary stress. Jasper also realized that other students in the class had been impacted by

DOI: 10.4324/9781003717232-9

this document's design. A few students had been assisting their peer to help her understand the material, which had impacted class discussions and group work. Others had missing assignments, and he wondered if that, too, could be traced back to the syllabus design. Similarly, the time Jasper would need to make the essential changes to the document and then meet with the student to help her catch up would take away from his other work.

Jasper learned that not only did he need to revise his document, he also needed to find ways to assess the functionality of his documents. Asking for feedback, for instance, would have provided him with different user perspectives. Reflecting on how his audience would engage with his document, where they would access it, and what they would use it for would have helped him identify the assumptions he had when creating his document in the first place. This step may have also offered opportunities for him to address those assumptions and eliminate possible challenges in the organization and design. In other words, using a range of **assessment** practices would have enabled Jasper to redesign his syllabus to include, among other things, a simplified layout, a color palette that passed a contrast ratio test, and alt text for the decorative icons and images.

Jasper's experience serves as an example of why reflectively assessing our documents should go beyond just troubleshooting. Most if not all of us assess as part of our daily work. We teach in classrooms and meeting spaces, online learning platforms, and public-facing venues. We work with assignments, research, professional materials, and institutional structures, all requiring our assessment. We know that best practices indicate that assessment should be a deliberate rhetorical act that invites us to consider the assumptions and the stories that shape the product's content, form, and structure. Reflective assessment is about recognizing all the contexts and ways in which our documents will be accessed and used. Becoming more aware of how our design decisions can exclude participation happens when we conduct assessments. It is only through these that we can confirm that our documents are successful.

And yet, assessment can take on many different forms and can happen at any point in the design process. It should be framed as an ongoing means for transforming our ideas and our documents into better meaning-making experiences for all. So far in this book, you participated in several assessment experiences, from analyzing the usefulness of your document's genre features to asking your colleagues for written feedback on your designs. Beyond this book, consider other ways you've engaged in assessment. Have you asked someone to read aloud a draft of a cover letter before you sent it? Have you gone into a writing center and asked for help with tone or clarity? Have you worked with GenAI to reorganize an outline for readability? For many of us, we engage in assessment practices often. Sometimes, it's as simple as listening to a reader and reflecting on how to meet their needs. Sometimes, it's more complex and might involve a focus group or short survey. Whether you have different users interact with a first draft or are conducting a focus group on a close-to-finished draft, you can discern why and how something is working or isn't by listening and reflecting on your users' experiences. Building on these instances, this chapter provides additional ways in which we might assess whether we are on the right track with our design decisions so that our final product best serves our purposes and those of our users.

In Part II of this book, we've attempted to answer the question: How does one go from brainstorming the most (and sometimes wildest) possible ideas for a document to turning in a final draft? Or, *how do we develop a document from divergent imagining to convergent design*? Answering such a question has revealed to us opportunities for making a multitude of design choices. Yet, to know if any or all of those choices work, we must use assessment. Whether that assessment happens in the midst of divergence or convergence, or somewhere in between, assessment can create transformative spaces, and it's those spaces that are the subject of this chapter.

6.1 Story

Foremost, design assessment must engage **story**. Story is the where and how the meaning of a document is made and understood, and it is constructed through its rhetorical situation: the interactions of the writer, the document itself, its users, and the context in which it lives. Not only is story created in these interactions as they occur, but our documents are shaped by past stories too—from the stories of ourselves as designers to the stories of users. These stories, those of ourselves and those of our users, are also shaped by the contexts in which we design and use documents. Places and spaces (which have their own stories) contribute to our document's story as well. In fact, documents themselves have complex histories, ones that are shaped by evolving genres and their changing conventions. After all, genres are not static; they change over time to reflect our cultures, politics, materials, power dynamics, and technology.

So, to make our documents usable and accessible (more on this later), we must recognize these stories and come back to them often. This coming back, this act of acknowledgment and reflection if you will, is what makes assessment successful. Indeed, it helps us to reframe our design practices as storytelling. We might ask in assessment, for instance: What stories do our documents need to tell? How will our documents acknowledge and engage our users' stories?

Jasper's syllabus told his student, for instance, that her story hadn't been considered, that his course was for students whose bodies didn't need to rely on a screen reader. This was, we hope, not the story Jasper had intended to tell, but one that he ultimately did.

Framing our documents as meaning-making devices (i.e., stories) shaped by people and places and their experiences can reveal opportunities for powerful transformations. In fact, it can help us push back against exclusionary practices. That's because in reflective assessment, not only do we determine what is working and what is not, we also craft a plan for revision, which can include envisioning a new story for our document.

Too often conventions, be they related to assessment, design, content, or genre, reflect dominant cultural and social power dynamics and expectations. Developing socially just conventions, those that instigate or sustain equity regardless of the social constructs and physical and material realities users exist within, requires us to actively acknowledge, understand, and seek ways to support and validate lived experiences that are marginalized, silenced, or erased. Developing socially just conventions requires that we listen to stories that "challenge traditional power structures and [promote] inclusivity" (Aldana, 2024, p. 15).

Counterstory, in its most basic sense is an alternative narrative. It ranges from a different approach or structure to an entirely different perspective, often one that is silenced by a metanarrative or dominant power dynamic. In many disciplines, including RCWS, scholars have identified the power of counterstory in making space for and giving voice to experience that does not align with hegemonic narratives (e.g., see Aldana, 2024; Bell, 2008/1970; Collins, 2019; Inoue, 2015; Martinez, 2020; Powell, 2002; Solórzano and Yosso, 2002). In the humanities, counterstory is both methodology and method (Martinez). It is a way for us to understand experience and to share it. Importantly, counterstory can function as an organizing facet throughout our academic lives, including our administrative work, teaching, research, service, community building, assessment, civic initiatives, public-facing representation, and social engagement.

To demonstrate how assessment through story and counterstory can lead us to **transformative design** practices, which focus on creating equitable, inclusive, sustainable designs, we can point to the common practice of evaluating faculty performance and the documents that this involves. As often is the case, this evaluation can present us with challenging design choices especially when our professional activity does not quite translate into the traditional institutional expectations of the documents they instruct us to submit for that evaluation.

For example, when it comes to research and scholarship, often tenure, promotion, meritorious awards, and contract renewal decisions reward a finished product, which usually means you've published research or scholarship, presented at a conference, facilitated highly specialized workshops, or something similar. Whatever that finished product is that you provide the reviewer(s) to assess, it more often than not fails to capture all the work involved in completing it. The "invisible" work, the drafting, data collection, revising, collaborations, knowledge making, and so on, is rarely represented in ways that are explicit and recognizable across disciplines and beyond the intimacy of the work you've done. What academic professionals do to get published or to present often gets reduced to one line on a CV or a few sentences in a promotion application or portfolio narrative. That one CV line and those few sentences do not tell the story of the weeks, months, even years of the day-to-day work, that is, it does not make our labor visible. After all, how do these brief textual samples tell a review committee of the hours spent hovering over a keyboard typing up draft after draft, or the time it took to prepare countless emails trying to coordinate our research with stakeholders? Or what it took to complete the Institutional Review Board (IRB) applications or the funding applications before that research even started? How do you communicate the impact your work has on specific communities through a title on your CV? Instead, this line on your CV or the few sentences in your promotion application or portfolio get reduced to a somewhat generic story, or stock story, often built on what has been deemed a dominant standard for privileged bodies, one used to evaluate whether a faculty member has enough of the right work to be considered for tenure, promotion, merit pay, and/or contract renewal.

In their work on reviewing student writing, Stephanie West-Puckett, Nicole I. Caswell, and William P. Banks (2023) highlight how stock stories fail to recognize unique bodies and the work they do when writing. Their findings helped them "to better understand the invisible labor that certain bodies have had to engage with in writing cultures that were not built with them in mind" (p. 198). We can draw parallels between their critique of the ways in which institutions currently review writing students and the ways in which institutions currently review faculty work. Like students, faculty activity is often evaluated against a stock story. In the moments when we're applying for jobs or promotion, or when we're going through a review of any kind, we are likely asked to list products in a particular type of document according to a strict set of guidelines that don't tell the whole story of the work we have done to produce them.

What West-Puckett, Caswell, and Banks suggest, and what we may want to take up as faculty who are being evaluated on our work's products, is that we find ways that allow us to tell a counterstory with our documents. Current evaluation practices focus on finished products, which West-Puckett, Caswell, and Banks believe limits institutions, disciplines, and faculty understanding of the real experiences of how work gets accomplished. Drawing on a cultural rhetorics framework, they argue that counterstories allow the work to be humanized (p. 199).

This applies across the vast range of documents we create and engage as academics. If we want socially just conventions, humanizing the work of the designer and of the user must remain at the locus of every step. Just as empathy is the grounding tenet of design thinking and access drives information architecture, we argue that counterstory is the heart of assessing usability.

6.2 Usability and Accessibility

Our primary objective with document design assessment is to render our documents usable and accessible. The terms usability and accessibility, however, are not the same, and the distinction between them is an important one. **Usability** refers to whether a user can use a document effectively to achieve their intended goals. Put differently, users come to a document for a reason (often it is to learn information), and the usability of the document helps them reach this goal by ensuring they can navigate, understand, and interact with the document in ways that meet their needs. Document usability frequently relies on the quality of the information architecture, which helps ensure that users will face few challenges or problems engaging with the document in ways that meet its purpose.

Accessibility refers to whether all users, regardless of ability, can understand (or access) a document. For example, accessibility should make certain that all users, not just some, can interact with and perceive your document in meaningful ways. Douglas Eyman (2016) writes that "Access/ibility is a rhetorical process" in which you "consider the audiences (scholarly or public) and their motivations for accessing your text" (n.p.). While usability is about effectiveness and efficiency, accessibility is about fairness and inclusion. When you use both in your documents, you ensure that your design will likely work for everyone.

Critically, both usability and accessibility require an awareness of cultural, social, and economic constructs; that is, context that exists beyond the physical text. These constructs can impact how a user engages a text, how much time it takes to find and gather information, variations in what that information means or how it is applied, and so on. This context helps us better understand and plan the **user experience (UX)**. Donald Norman (2004), who is often credited with coining the term, argues that user experience includes "function, performance, and usability" (p. 37). UX includes many of the considerations we've addressed throughout this book. Affordances, feedback, and iterations, for instance, are key elements in designing useful, functional products (in our case, we're focused on documents). UX considers the entirety of the user's journey with a text, not just reading it or viewing it, but how they come to it, what they do with it, and if and how they repeat their use.

Earlier in this book, you learned that you, as a writer, play an important role in the writing process. Yet, because we each have biases and assumptions, informed by our histories and backgrounds, an important step in assessing whether our documents are usable and accessible involves moving beyond ourselves and observing how others experience documents. Addressing the user's experience does more than answer the question, "Is the document's flow supporting the user's cognitive process?" Experience considerations in design usability and accessibility attend to questions such as: Does the time needed to use the document align culturally with how users read and interpret? Does the language of the document assume everyone, including those translating or coming from different cultures, will understand your intention? And, do your users have the technology necessary to read and interact with the document? User experience is, in part, deeply empathetic. It seeks to understand the user as a whole person and their interaction with the document as a whole experience.

In the example earlier in this chapter of Jasper's syllabus, it is clear that Jasper had not asked or answered such questions. His experience shows us that assessment of our document's usability and accessibility must consider how and where users will engage our documents. Because his student would need a screen reader, Jasper's document (which wasn't designed for such a technology) was not usable or accessible. Awareness of who users are and analyzing their experience helps designers address their own biases and assumptions and helps identify constraints that have perhaps been overlooked.

Jasper had assumed that his students would use and access his syllabus in much the same way he did. He assumed his own constraints to be the only constraints. Sometimes, when we aren't sure what our users' experiences may be, or even who our users are, beginning with our own experience can be a helpful way to establish assessment criteria and standards. Our own points of engagement can become areas to explore and envision differently. In aiming for a professional and inviting syllabus, the icons Jasper chose may have logically reflected different sections of his document. But, how much of that logic is bound to his experience? Let's say he chose as an icon for "assignments" a line drawing of a page (a rectangle with a few horizontal lines stacked throughout its height) because his experiences as a student included frequently submitting physical pages of work. Students viewing the syllabus in a digital space might see the icon and assume it's a hyperlink to a site with the assignment descriptions or perhaps it's supposed to lead them to a portal where they submit their work. Or, if Jasper's assignments include discussions and collaborative activities, the single page might be confusing or seem like an illogical choice. Still other students may have never experienced submitting assignments in physical forms and could be altogether confused by the association. While the latter seems unlikely to either of us writing this text, we wonder how much of that assumption is our own bias showing up in this book.

TABLE 6.1 Activity: Identifying your Assumptions

For this activity, you will try to identify your own assumptions that may be hidden in your design and in your content. Select one of your professional documents that has a relatively sizable audience. Ideally, you will choose a document that has at least 10-12 people. For example, you may choose a syllabus, course assignment, CV, research proposal, or philosophy statement (i.e., teaching, diversity, research, or administrative statement).

Content Assumptions:

First, imagine you are talking to someone unfamiliar with your discipline (or with academic culture altogether). Read your document to this unfamiliar user. Identify when something seems like it would need additional explanation or when something comes up that would be unfamiliar. Circle or highlight the text. After reading the complete document, return to the identified content and note how you might provide better context or make the meaning clear to the unfamiliar user.

Next, keeping that same audience member in mind, write a letter to the user and provide brief summaries of each section and/or paragraph of the document to help them understand the purpose and meaning of each part. Identify where the summaries overlap with existing content and note when the summaries provide additional information such as context clues or clarified content to help your unfamiliar user.

Take a break from this document; we recommend at least an hour. When you return to it, read with resistance. Question every claim made in the document and analyze the language used throughout it. Ask "why" and "how" when directions are provided or accomplishments are included. Keeping empathy in mind, question the value of information (i.e., "Why does this matter?" and "Why do I care?").

Finally, review the materials you have generated in the above steps and create a log of your assumptions. Account for how your assumptions appeared in the text and the impact each assumption could have on the user and on you. This log could be a simple list, or it can be a more developed record.

(*Continued*)

TABLE 6.1 (Continued)

Design Assumptions:

To test design assumptions, we encourage you to consider how your document is most likely going to be used. The following activity assumes you are working with a digital document. You can adapt or change the steps for a physical document. *We have provided an alternative for printed documents in italicized text below each step in the following part of this activity.*

First, open your document in the digital space you assume your user will also view it. For example, you may open your CV in a PDF reader. Zoom to a full-page view and note whether the text remains coherent (readable) within the design. Identify how your eye moves through the design: what elements you notice first, second, and so on; where you pause or stop; if/when you get confused on where to look next.

Then, zoom in. Enlarge the document to 300% or more. How does this affect the way you read the document? Do you get lost moving from one line to the next? From one section to the next? Are headings and subheadings easily identifiable at this size? It may be helpful to explore this part of the activity at several different sizes; if you started at 300%, try 500% and notice differences. Make a few notes on your experience.

To adapt this part of the activity, you might print your document at 100% and again with an enlarged print scale.

Next, listen to your design for clarity and coherence. If your application does not offer adaptive solutions like a screen reader, find an app that will read your document aloud. What parts of your document are skipped over? What parts are read in the wrong order?

To adapt this part of the activity, you might print your document in color and again in grayscale. This is helpful to determine how reliant you are on color to communicate your message, for example.

Then, copy the content of your document into a plain text editor, such as Notepad or TextEdit. In the editor application, make sure you have removed all text formatting from your copied content (i.e., you should be viewing a "plain text" version of your document). Is your document still readable? Can you determine what content is a heading or subheading?

To adapt this part of the activity, turn your printed copies upside down and see if the design information remains coherent. Consider the design structure and ask questions like: Are the sections and subsections still obvious? Do the headings still register as headings? How does white space impact the design?

Finally, these actions are a starting point to help you identify a few potential assumptions that may be embedded in your designs. They can help you realize when and how you are relying on design content to communicate your message and may help you identify challenges your design creates for users. As you did with the content assumptions, create a log of the design assumptions you identified and the potential impact these could have on your document's users. Note how you might avoid these in future designs and how you can eliminate them in your current documents.

Identifying our own assumptions can be a difficult starting point. If you're struggling, seek out a document that you can work with that is similar to the one you chose for this activity but authored by someone else. It can be helpful to look at a similar document in a different discipline (i.e., a CV in a different field) or a similar document written for a different audience (i.e., a syllabus for a different course level). After completing the activity, return to your own document and repeat the steps.

Importantly, while identifying assumptions and constraints can be a useful way to begin developing parameters for testing usability and accessibility, critical design assessment isn't a checklist to be used after our document has been drafted to accommodate people who might be different from us. In other words, designing for usability is an ongoing process that begins with empathy and a recognition of what makes a document usable and accessible to all. Do not simply wait until the document is complete and then add accessible features like alternative text (i.e., alt text) and a readable font. Seek a range of testing mechanisms that offer varied perspectives so that we make sure we don't rely on our own biased assumptions to guide our design choices. According to Sean Zdenek (2020), "When we take access and inclusion seriously, whether in the classroom, the workplace, or on the web, we reconsider fundamental assumptions—assumptions that have typically privileged the perspectives and values of nondisabled 'default users' (Yergeau et al.) to the exclusion of people with disabilities" (p. 536). There are no "normal" users for our documents; therefore, when we create a document, we should not start by envisioning a "normal" user. Doing this puts us in the same position as Jasper and sets us up to fail our users.

Instead, we should consider how the document will be used by diverse bodies. Returning to the rhetorical situation here can be useful, especially if you focus on the purpose of the document and the context(s) in which it will exist. If your document is digital, consider all the different technologies that may be used to access the information it contains. If your document is a website, users might access it on a desktop computer, laptop, tablet, phone, television, or even a gaming device. Likewise, users may have adaptive devices with which your website needs to fluidly interact. They may not have access to color differences, or their technology may not read specific types of script or code. If your document will circulate in a digital space and a physical space, some typography choices may not work as well in one environment as in the other, and some design choices (such as color or graphics) may not print well. We also read differently in digital environments than we do in physical spaces, which can impact how much text you can place together on a page, for example. Therefore, we must carefully review the contexts in which our users will use our documents and use this information to design and revise our documents.

6.3 Testing Document Designs

If you have ever conducted primary research, many of the following methods may already be familiar to you. If you find this is the case, it may be helpful for you to conceptualize testing as research you are conducting on your document. Just as our choice of research protocol depends greatly on the purpose, population, and timeline of the project we are working on, our document testing protocol will depend similarly on our document's context.

To begin, sharing your document and asking users to follow a think-aloud protocol may garner insight into how your users interact with and understand your document. A think-aloud protocol means that users verbalize their thoughts in real time while they are interacting with your document to complete a goal all while you, the designer, take notes. For example, say you write a teaching philosophy statement that you hope to use in a job application. The job ad states that the institution is looking for someone who can teach in a fast-paced, technology-enriched environment that puts students at the center of the classroom. To test the statement you wrote, you ask a colleague to read it out loud and verbalize their reactions. As you listen to your colleague, you make notes about what causes them to stumble, to stop and go back and reread, or to ponder a question or two. These data you gathered serve as an aid to help you reflect on your document's readability and flow. You might ask yourself, how did my colleague construct meaning as they moved from sentence to sentence, paragraph to paragraph, section to section?

TABLE 6.2 Activity: Think-Aloud Test

Choose a document that you have recently designed. Have a colleague read it out loud to you and verbalize their thoughts as they do. As your colleague reads this document and verbalizes their thoughts, make notes about what you are hearing and observing. In addition to noting what they say about the document, consider the following points of interest:

- What changes do you notice in your colleague's tone of voice, posture, and facial expressions as they read?
- When do they slow their reading or stumble over words or navigation (i.e., not knowing where to go next)?
- What emotional responses register as they engage your document?

It may be helpful to record your reader if you're concerned that you won't effectively capture their experience with notes.

Remember that reflection is vital to successful usability testing, both from you and from your test audience. After the think-aloud protocol is complete, ask your reader to provide some final thoughts and be sure to reflect on these notes as you plan your document's revision (i.e., iteration).

Another form of testing is to interview your colleague. Though you can pair interviewing with think-aloud testing, you can use this protocol independently. Interviews essentially allow you to have a conversation about your text. You could ask direct questions as to what your colleague found frustrating, helpful, and/or confusing. You could ask content-driven questions like "Did I adequately show I can work in a technology-enriched environment?" and design-driven questions like "How long did it take you to determine the reading direction (or orientation)?" One of the more profound advantages to interviewing is that it allows you to also prompt your colleague to ask their own questions. Perhaps, they might ask you why you wrote "x" as opposed to "y" or why you chose to use color for specific elements of the document.

It should be noted that interviews don't always have to take place after your colleague reads your document. Asking users questions about the document genre, content, and functionality before they've read your document can help you identify how they prioritize expectations and assumptions. Pausing in the middle of your colleague's reading and asking questions can provide in-the-moment reflection that may get lost or forgotten as they continue their interaction. Determining when and how you will ask questions during the interview protocol is as important as developing the questions. So, plan ahead and determine what your goals are for interviewing in the first place and when and how you will conduct your interviews to best meet these goals.

TABLE 6.3 Activity: Interview

Choose a document that you have recently designed. This can be the same document you used in the previous activity or a different one. Before you have a colleague read it, write down 5-7 interview questions you have about the document that you could ask this colleague. Have a goal for asking these questions. What, in other words, do you wish to get out of asking them? The questions should be questions you don't already know the answer to or can't find the answer to on your own. They should also be clear and open-ended to give you the best chance for capturing usable data. Next, determine the best time to ask these questions (before, during, after your colleague reads your document) and then share your document with your colleague.

When you are confident your interview protocol is appropriately developed and planned, conduct your interview, making sure to take accurate notes and to ask follow-up questions when you need further information. You may find it helpful to record the interview if you feel your notes won't accurately capture the feedback.

After you conduct your interview, reflect on what you found and make a plan for revising this document based on the feedback. To help you begin reflecting on your findings from the interview, consider these questions:

- What categories could you develop to help you organize the feedback?
- What did your user appreciate in your document's design and/or content?
- What findings from your interview surprised you the most?
- Are there comments in the interview that you don't understand or disagree with? Do you need to ask a follow-up question for clarity?

A third testing option commonly used by document designers is a compare-and-contrast test, or competitive testing. With this method, you provide more than one version of your document and ask users to try each option, noting what they felt were the pros and cons among the versions. This can be helpful if you are experimenting with new forms of established genres, altering expected organization, or if you're unfamiliar with your user's behavior as they engage a particular type of document. For example, if you are redesigning your CV to represent your teaching activity as part of your research, you may need to develop two or three ways of organizing your content and then get feedback on them from users. You might ask a few peers to look at each option and identify which one provides the information in the most usable and accessible way.

TABLE 6.4 Activity: Multiple Versions

For this activity, choose one of the classes you are teaching and create three versions of an introductory paragraph for your class that you will share via the class's course management site. During the first week of classes, this statement will appear on the site as the first announcement and the introduction to you and your class. In other words, this is likely your first impression on your students. Because this will be a first impression, you might start by thinking about what priorities you want to highlight in the paragraph and what tone of voice would be best to do so.
Share the three versions with current or previous students who are familiar with your class. If this isn't possible, choose a few students whom you trust will give you honest feedback. Using a reflective protocol that best suits the content of the statement and your feedback needs (i.e., think aloud, interview, survey, tree testing, etc.), collect user responses that you can then use to determine the most viable version of your statement and plan your revisions accordingly.

Other tests you might consider include task-based tests, focus groups, and surveys. Task-based testing, such as tree tests or sorting, is useful if you need to test the information architecture of your document. For example, if you need to determine if your document's navigation is intuitive for users, you might create a tree test protocol asking users to identify how they move through the information using numbers that coordinate with when and how they access every element. Although this method won't necessarily explain why they make navigational choices, it can show you the sequence in which they access information and when or how often they return to information.

Focus groups and surveys are useful when you need feedback from a wide range of users or if your document will be used in collaborative settings. For example, if you design a report that will be referenced during planning meetings, a focus group can help you determine how a group will engage the report and what you can do to improve its functionality. Perhaps you determine that it is easier to share the report with others if it is spiral-bound or, if it can live digitally, when it is housed on a platform that permits real-time sharing among multiple users.

Before we move on to discussing what we do with the results of our tests, it merits attention that regardless of the type of test you use, in your planning for it, you should be conscious of your testers' time and labor. There comes a time when we may ask too much of our testers (a tipping point if you will) where their efforts become fatigued rendering them useless. This benefits no one and we should avoid this whenever possible.

Performing tests is an important form of assessment that can lead us to determine whether our documents will work and can help us plan ways for improving them. The examples we've offered here of testing our documents can serve as starting points. There are certainly other ways of testing that may be more beneficial for your purposes, and we hope you will explore them.

6.4 Revision as Design

Testing and the data we gather from it can help us plan and implement meaningful revisions for our documents. In fact, think of **revision** as design since it is an intentional iterative process of refinement to improve how a document works for everyone. In the act of revising, you re-envision what your document is and does; these revisions become iterations of your document. Developing iterations is a rhetorical act. As you revise, you once again work your way through the rhetorical situation, making decisions that more accurately reflect your audience, purpose, self, context, and text. Likewise, it enables you to work your way through the initial assumptions you had about these to ensure you have addressed them. When you revise, you empathize and you adapt.

As a rhetorical act, revisions will happen in different ways depending on what we find out in our assessments. We may find ourselves changing words as we develop an initial draft because we prefer the sound of one word over another or determine that a different word makes more sense than our original choice. Our approach to writing may take us through invention, drafting, and revision almost simultaneously. RCWS scholars refer to this as **recursive revision**, and it can help writers gain confidence in their drafts or propel them through particularly challenging writing situations. Recursive revision can include feedback, but it more commonly centers the writer by prioritizing their in-the-moment decisions. Recursive revision is akin to self-assessment in which we revisit our own stories and those that we wish to tell with our documents.

Responsive revision, on the other hand, prioritizes the reader and requires user feedback. In other words, as a writer, you will respond to the experiences that your users have when working with your document. Listening to them and then making changes to better serve their needs will ultimately make your document more user-friendly. Responsive revision is akin to "reading the room"; it is about situational awareness, being able to recognize how users are using your document and then making improvements that better serve them.

Recursive revision and responsive revision are not mutually exclusive, though, and many writers find they need to engage both throughout the development process, particularly when engaging in revision as part of transformative design. Clarifying your message (i.e., removing jargon, simplifying concepts), refining the visual appearance of your document (i.e., choosing a better hierarchy, spacing, headings), and safeguarding its functionality (i.e., confirming smooth navigation) are often direct pathways to equity and inclusion in document design and revision. These actions open up your document to as many users as possible.

If you've ever revised, you probably know that some revisions are easier than others. Sometimes in testing our documents, we might not collect the data we need. We may find we did not gather enough data or feedback, or we might collect too much; we might also find that we collect the wrong data and that the information available to us fails to address our revision needs. Regardless of our situation, if the feedback we're using does not match our purpose, we may find that we have created more work for ourselves and for those testing our designs. To reduce the chances of finding ourselves in such a situation, we must be strategic when planning our workflow and when setting our goals for testing.

However, if you find your design overwhelmed with data, one approach may mean circling back to a concept introduced earlier in this chapter, that of story and using that as a framework for interpreting your data. **Data storytelling** helps to communicate important narratives connected to (often) complex data so that the value and meaning of the information can be better understood. This might be a familiar concept to you if you have ever had to share the results of a research study you conducted. Researchers wanting to share their results might shape these into stories, narratives that make these data intelligible, especially to those who may be unfamiliar with them in the first place. Data storytelling, as Brent Dykes (2020) reminds us, can help our audience not just understand data or information but engage it (p. 26). So, if we find ourselves with an abundance of feedback data from testing our documents, we might think about shaping these data into stories that help us better understand them so that we can make better revision choices.

Coding data is yet another option for making data more manageable. In Chapter 5 you learned that coding helps you note patterns and eliminate redundancies. When this method of working with information is applicable, it provides a simplified view of (sometimes quite a lot of) data. For instance, instead of looking at every piece of data gathered in your user tests, you would look at categories of information, groups that include a smaller set of data. With your data organized in this way, you can more easily identify the parts of your document that you need to prioritize in the next iteration. This approach may also make visible to you any conflicting user feedback you may have collected. While those conflicts may seem dismissible, often they can represent user differences and can help you enhance usability and accessibility in your design.

You may find it helpful to chart or map out your priorities so that you can plan how you address them. While this approach is helpful with any size or type of document, it can be particularly useful with longer documents and sustained projects, such as promotion dossiers or publications.

The chart in Table 6.5 outlines a revision workflow that we have found useful in some of our previous projects. You are welcome to use our structure, or you may want to develop one of your own. The goal with this chart is to discern how much effort is needed to address the revisions your document requires and identify when and how the revisions will occur.

TABLE 6.5 Revision Workflow Chart

What is the design problem or user need?	Why is it a problem or need?	Where does the problem or need occur?	How will revision address this?	At what stage (in iteration development) will this be addressed?	How long will this revision take to complete?	How important is this revision?

Lastly, remember that creating different iterations of the same content, or repurposing content for different audiences and contexts, is common to any professional setting and occurs across all disciplines throughout academia. For example, you might have a two-page CV for publication or grant applications and a 12-page CV for performance reviews or applying for jobs. A new program proposal will likely have iterations for department faculty, marketing and public relations staff, and institutional effectiveness and academic review boards. A course syllabus may have iterations for institutional circulation and archiving, course management platforms, student reference, and teacher-research projects. Keep in mind that revision isn't just about perfecting a single document; it is about capitalizing on all the possibilities or iterations for that document.

6.5 Benefits of Failure

In the story that begins this chapter, it is clear that Jasper and thus his document had failed to consider all of his users. This is an example of productive failure, however, because it led Jasper to learn and grow as a designer. No matter how much we plan, sometimes our documents will fail. That is okay; it's even encouraged. Importantly, failure helps us acknowledge why, where, and when to make changes in our processes, practices, content, and beyond. Failure, therefore, can be considered a productive iteration and is often considered a vital part of design thinking.

WHAT AI HAS TO SAY:

Failure in document design can actually be a powerful learning tool. Here are some key benefits:

Reveals User Needs
When a design fails—maybe readers misunderstand the content or struggle with navigation—it highlights gaps between the designer's assumptions and the audience's actual needs. This feedback is invaluable for creating more user-centered documents.

Encourages Iterative Improvement
Failure often sparks revision. It pushes designers to test, refine, and experiment with layout, typography, and structure. This iterative process usually leads to stronger, more effective designs.

Builds Problem-Solving Skills
Encountering design flaws forces you to analyze why something didn't work—was it hierarchy, readability, accessibility? This critical thinking strengthens your ability to anticipate and prevent similar issues in future projects.

Promotes Creativity
Constraints and setbacks often lead to innovative solutions. When a design fails, you're more likely to explore unconventional approaches or rethink your visual strategy.

Deepens Understanding of Design Principles
Failure makes abstract principles (like contrast, alignment, proximity) tangible. Seeing what happens when these principles are ignored reinforces their importance.

Improves Communication and Collaboration
Sharing and discussing design failures with peers or stakeholders fosters transparency and collaboration. It helps teams align on goals and learn collectively.

Code Credit: Microsoft, *Copilot* (2025, December 4)

> This overview offers a few common benefits but seems limited in its scope. It seems to assume that failure occurs after the design in completed. Based on your own experience, what would you add to this list to represent failure that occurs at different times throughout the design process?

> We appreciate the final two points emphasizing tangibility and transparency. Design is a collaboration between the developer(s) and the user(s). And, the desing choices we make may seem abstract but are often impactful, concrete parts of the user experience.

Example of an AI output generated with the prompt: "Explain how failure in document design can be a learning tool. Provide a bulleted list of key benefits with brief explanations." Code Credit: Microsoft, *Copilot* (2025, December 4).

Henry Petroski (2018) notes, "Whenever we use some *thing* to do *something* we expect it to do, we test it. [...] Failures are remarkable. The failures always teach us more than the successes about the design of things" (p. 48).

Failure often encourages better iterations at every stage of the design process. Building on the output included in the "What AI Has to Say" example, when we fail early and often, we are positioned to recursively revise, to repeatedly revisit the stories that inform our designs and our documents, to listen differently to our users, to think differently about our products. That is, it can be a chance for us to produce better iterations of our documents, iterations that take into consideration what we missed in previous versions.

6.6 Scenario: Testing and Revising Website Design

For this scenario, imagine you are tasked with revising your department's website. Your university has an office that maintains the institution's website, and they have requested faculty input to help create a robust representation of specific programs and departments. You are asked to review your department's webpages, which have not been updated in five years and are outdated, and provide suggestions and content for the revision. After reviewing the webpages and establishing feedback, you and a small committee of peers will develop new content, update existing materials, and identify new assets (photos, content categories, tools, etc.) that the office has requested.

TABLE 6.6 Activity: Revising from Start to Finish

After you locate your department's website (or webpage), explore it and make your own observations of it, writing them down in clear and accurate notes. You might consider your first impressions, the purpose for the website, and how navigable it is to start with.

Next, test the current website with others to learn more about how and why other users use it. Likely, there are several different users: students, faculty, staff, administrators, alumni, potential students, donors, and/or curious members of the public. Choose one of these audiences and using the information in this chapter, conduct one of the following tests with them:

- Think-aloud protocol
- Interview
- Task-based tests
- Focus group
- Survey

As you conduct your test, make sure to adequately collect data on your findings. Take notes and/or record the interaction and complete an initial reflection on the user feedback.

Then, sort through these data more methodically and reflect on them. Code or map the data appropriately so that you can prioritize which problems need to be addressed first, second, and so forth and why.

If you have time, repeat this activity with another user and/or a different test protocol. Say, for instance, if you chose to test with a staff member the first time, try conducting the same test with a student. You could then compare your findings, noting the different needs of different users.

Finally, develop a plan for your revisions by writing out each step you will take along with a justification. Share this plan with a colleague who is familiar with your department's website.

The new content must align with the website's brand and organization template and with your department's activities, mission, curricula, and people.

6.7 Resistance and Transformation

Revision is the location where convergent design happens and where resistance to exclusionary conventions becomes a means for transformation. More pointedly, we believe that convergent design's end goal is to resist long-standing practices and conventions that fail to account for difference, regardless of what that difference may be. Revision isn't about simply correcting; it is about making powerful changes through smart, ethical design decisions.

Some may see this as resistance, but we see this as transformation. Beyond functionality, all design—be it a one-page program description or a lunar module—should reflect socially just conventions and keep visible diverse experiences and stories. Throughout this book we have at times offered concrete directions to guide your convergent design practices and at times, we have been purposefully abstract. We hope you have worked through the activities in this book and applied the knowledge and skills you've honed to documents specific to your experience, to your story. You are the designer. You make the choices. You create the changes.

6.8 Chapter 6 Summary

This chapter's focus on transforming documents through assessment, testing, and revision can help designers craft documents that work for everyone. Indeed, when designers gather feedback on their documents, they are better positioned to reshape them into their best versions. Key takeaways from this chapter include:

- assessment requires rhetorical reflection and uncovering the stories our documents tell and don't tell;
- assessing and testing from a place of counterstory can facilitate socially just designs that push back on exclusionary practices and better represent diverse voices;
- testing for usability and accessibility facilitates ensuring everyone can access a document and use it effectively without unnecessary challenges.

References

Aldana, Adriana. (2024). Counterstory pedagogy: Student letters of resilience, healing, and resistance. *Elon University Center for Engaged Learning*. https://doi.org/10.36284/celelon.oa8

Bell, Derrick. (2008). *Race, racism, and American law*, 6th ed. Aspen (originally published in 1970).

Collins, Patricia Hill. (2019). *Intersectionality and critical social theory*. Duke University Press.

Dykes, Brent. (2020). *Effective data storytelling: How to drive change with data, narrative and visuals*. Wylie.

Eyman, Douglas. (Ed.). (2016). Access/ibility: Access and usability for digital publishing. *Kairos: A Journal of Rhetoric, Technology, and Pedagogy*, *20*(2). https://kairos.technorhetoric.net/20.2/topoi/eyman-et-al/.

Inoue, Asao. (2015). *Anitracist writing assessment ecologies*. WAC Clearinghouse; University of Colorado Press.

Martinez, Aja. (2020). *Counterstory: The rhetoric and writing of critical race theory*. NCTE.

Microsoft. (2025, December 4). *Copilot* [Large Language Model]. https://copilot.microsoft.com

Norman, Donald. (2004). *Emotional design: Why we love (or hate) everyday things*. Basic Books.

Petroski, Henry. (2018). *Success through failure: The paradox of design*. Princeton University Press.

Powell, Malea. (2002). Rhetorics of survivance: How American Indians use writing. *College Composition and Communication*, *53*(3), 396–434.

Solórzano, Daniel G., & Yosso, Tara Y. (2002). Critical race methodology: Counter-storytelling as an analytical framework in education research. *Qualitative Inquiry*, *8*(1), 23–44. https://doi.org/10.1177/107780040200800103

West-Puckett, Stephanie, Caswell, Nicole I., & Banks, William P. (2023). Engaging assessment counterstories through a cultural rhetorics framework. *College Composition and Communication*, *75*(1), 186–203.

Zdenek, Sean. (2020). Transforming access and inclusion in composition studies and technical communication. *College English*, *82*(5), 536–544.

APPENDIX A

Activities

The following activities help you to work through and reimagine your professional documents, asking you to pay close attention to how you design them and for whom you design them. We encourage you to apply what you have learned about rhetorical thinking, design thinking, information architecture, and technology as you reflect on what makes documents usable and accessible.

A.1 Mapping Your Job Portfolio

Whether you are applying for a new position or a promotion, you will likely need to create and/or revise your job portfolio (often referred to as a review portfolio, promotion portfolio, or a dossier). Job portfolios include a range of documents and require strategic, rhetorical design thinking. Since the portfolio's purpose is ultimately persuasive, it's important to make opportunities to spotlight your strengths and accomplishments. If you are creating documents like a CV or teaching philosophy using traditional genre conventions, you might map out these strengths in a storyboard like Table A.1.

This storyboard sketch illustrates how each of the documents in your portfolio can do something different. However, this approach might best serve those who can capture what they are about and what they have done using particular genre conventions, such as a research agenda or a teaching philosophy. The standard documents represented in Table A.1 might not fully serve your needs. For instance, we could argue that these genres traditionally privilege some and exclude others.

TABLE A.1 Portfolio Themes

Cover Letter or Summary	Curriculum Vitae	Teaching Philosophy or Statement	Statement of Diversity
Creative pedagogue with a student-centered classroom	Curriculum designer and innovator	Instructor who values rhetorical thinking	Promoting equity and inclusion in learning, service, and administration
Research agenda	**Sample syllabi**	**Sample assignments**	**Evidence**
Teacher-researcher who studies classroom best practices	Composition class that demonstrates a range of activities and assignments	A multimodal writing project for diverse audiences	Selected representation of research and service illustrating equity and inclusion, student-centeredness, and innovation

For this activity, think about your work and various expectations that you need to account for in your portfolio. Consider your professional and academic work—your teaching and research, your service, your contribution to your field and to your community—as well as your institution's expectations for job portfolio materials and materials encouraged by your discipline. Write a quick statement for each document that identifies what you will highlight in each one. Then, consider how you will work with or against the traditional genre conventions to best represent yourself within each document. Consider where in the portfolio review documents the audience might be open to new approaches and how altering genre conventions might better serve your work and your message.

A.2 Reimagining a Cover Letter

Cover letters are often opportunities to introduce yourself, a project, or an idea to a new audience, one with whom you are likely less familiar than, say, your colleagues down the hall. Cover letter audiences may be wholly unfamiliar. Because of this, empathizing with the audience and developing an understanding of what they need from the letter can be helpful. For this same reason, straying from convention in a cover letter can be scary.

Figure A.1 offers an example of a traditional cover letter written by someone replying to a job advertisement. As you read the example letter, note how this applicant identifies herself, her purpose, and what she perceives are her audience's priorities.

Mia Alcero

3421 NE 45th Street Miami, FL 33021 – (555) 555-5555 – malcero@hschool.edu

Oct. 4, 2023

7612 Bay Drive
North Bay, CA 90239

Dear Mr. George and the Bay State Hiring Committee:

I am writing to apply for the writing center coordinator and first-year composition instructor position as posted on Sept. 29, 2023, on your website. My work with writing centers and first-year composition students coupled with my graduate education will enable me to not only succeed but thrive in such a position.

Last year, I was appointed Assistant Director of the Writing Center at Holt University. During my first semester, I worked with the staff, students, and the director to implement a new training program aimed at making the consultation experiences better for both students and tutors. The program was specifically designed to give more agency to students through a series of self-prompted activities prior to and during each consultation. In other words, this program put students in the driver seat. This strategy proved effective and our writing center soon saw an increase in appointments and an increase in positive feedback. After this training program's success, I turned my attention to writing instructors in the next semester and offered up workshops to help them integrate writing center pedagogy in their classrooms, especially one-on-one conferencing with students. This is something I hope to implement at Bay State as I can see many similarities in the work I am doing with the instructors at my current institution and the work your instructors are doing at Bay State, particularly in the Writing Studio.

Drawing on my writing center experiences, I developed and taught a number of student-centered first-year writing courses that prepare students for the diverse writing they will do in college and beyond. Specifically, my courses enable students to think rhetorically and critically about a variety of texts, practice writing in different genres and modes, and work one-on-one with me to address their strengths and weaknesses. Using small group activities where students exchange drafts and discuss their work, read and analyze examples, and workshop their ideas, my courses are hands-on.

In addition to serving as the Assistant Director of the Writing Center, I have also served my institution in several ways. For two years, I served as the Chair of the First-Year Writing Committee. During that time, I worked to revise our curriculum to better ensure diverse forms of writing were valued throughout our program. We expanded the types of assignments to include more non-traditional work and encouraged our students to use their authentic voices.

Because I see myself as a teacher/researcher, much of my scholarship studies the practices that take place in writing centers and first-year writing classrooms. Last year, I studied training programs in writing centers by doing field observations and interviews. The result of this study led me to develop the training program I mentioned earlier in this letter. To build upon this study further, I would like to next study the lasting impacts this program has. I will be conducting an additional round of observations and interviews next year.

FIGURE A.1 Cover letter example.

This cover letter illustrates a conventional approach to the (US-based) academic job application cover letter.

(Continued)

I have also served my community in many ways. In 2020, I was successful in helping to secure funding for a local non-profit organization. Along with another volunteer, I wrote two grants and also created a number of recruitment materials to help this non-profit grow. After doing this, I invited the non-profit to visit my first-year writing classes to show my students how writing can make an impact on our communities. I think making community connections is important to my role as an instructor and hope to build partnerships with those in the Bay State community.

Thank you for your consideration. I look forward to meeting with the committee at your convenience. I would be happy to answer any questions or to set up an interview. You can reach me at 555-555-5555.

Sincerely,

Mia Alcero

FIGURE A.1 (Continued)

Now, reimagine Mia's cover letter for the job ad in Section 4.4 of Chapter 4. What could Mia do differently to ensure she stands out among the other job candidates for this job ad? How could applying lateral thinking and divergent design practices help her? What risks should she take?

Share your reimagined cover letter with a peer and ask them to provide a first impression. Compare this with the impression you had wanted to give with this reimagined letter. Did your peer have the impression you had intended to give? If so, why? What did you do right? If not, why? What could you change to more adequately reflect the impression you want to give?

A.3 Redesigning a Curriculum Vitae

For the following activity, reflect on what it means to write a curriculum vitae (CV) using the strategies of this book. To begin, analyze the traditional CV below and then answer the following questions. This CV was written by Mia Alcero, an RCWS faculty member who has experience teaching and researching writing. However, working through this activity can help you determine what's best for your own CV even if you are not an RCWS faculty member yourself and instead work in a different discipline.

1. What are your first impressions of this CV example? What stories does this CV tell about Mia?
2. Would the CV example work for you? That is, if you were to use a similar structure and organization as well as content, would you have a CV that works for you, or would you find this type of CV limiting?
3. What would you do differently and why? Would you, for example, reframe the service section into something different? Would you move the scholarship sections of publications and presentations and workshops higher up on the CV?

4. How could you revise Mia's CV to better show she is someone who values research? Someone who is a collaborator? Imagining different versions of this CV might help you to imagine different versions of your own CV.
5. What additional information or sections should Mia include if she were to apply for a tenure position at an R1 institution?
6. Based on what you reflected on in this activity, how might you approach redesigning your own CV?

Mia Alcero

3421 NE 45th Street, Miami, FL 33021 – (555) 555-5555 – malcero@hschool.edu

---

EDUCATION

Ph.D. in Composition and Rhetoric — Holt University (May 2022)
  Dissertation: Students Writing in the Writing Center
  committee members: John Galligan, Peter Bach, and Cindy Flack

M.A. in English — Kally University (May 2018)
  Certificate in the Teaching of Composition

B.A. in English — Kally University (May 2016)

ADMINISTRATIVE EXPERIENCE

Writing Center Assistant Director — Holt University (2021-Present)

- Plan and coordinate tutor training workshops once a month.
- Collect and manage writing center data and use it to best meet the needs of students.
- Assist the director with administrative tasks such as hiring tutors, meeting with faculty, and creating resources to be used in the writing center.

Writing Program Graduate Assistant — Holt University (2020-2021)

- Help adjunct instructors and graduate students prepare to teach composition courses.
- Visit writing program classrooms to ensure they are up-to-date with technology.
- Develop sample assignments and activities that can be used in writing program classrooms.

TEACHING EXPERIENCE

Instructor — Holt University (2021-Present)

ENG 101: Basic Writing

- Developed new assignments and activities for a themed basic writing course centered on writing for/in public spaces. Worked one-on-one with students using conferencing every four weeks to better address students' needs.

ENG 102: College Writing

- Created writing groups for students to work collaboratively on their writing. Invited professional writers to visit the classroom to speak about the writing they do as part of their careers.

ENG 230: Business Writing

- Partnered with a local small business so students could create real public facing documents.
- Invited professional writers to visit the classroom to speak about the writing they do as part of their careers.

Graduate Assistant/Instructor — Kally University (2017-2018)

WRIT 100: Basic Writing

- Provided hands-on writing workshops during class to help students brainstorm, revise, and edit their writing projects.

FIGURE A.2 CV example.

This illustrates a conventional approach to the (US-based) academic curriculum vitae.

(*Continued*)

SERVICE

Chair of First-Year Writing Committee, Holt University, 2020-2022.
- Revise curriculum for first-year writing courses.
- Review of program initiatives.

Writing Center Writing Group Leader, Holt University, 2020-2022.
- Organized weekly meetings for writing groups.
- Planned and executed Writing Week for undergraduate students.

Dean's Roundtable, Holt University, 2021.
- Met regularly with dean and colleagues to discuss college's needs.
- Worked with groups to meet college's goals each semester.

Grant Writer and Volunteer, South Trails Organization, 2020
- Co-wrote two grants to secure funding for the non-profit organization's trails institutive.
- Developed recruitment materials to recruit new volunteers to help with community outreach.

University Reading Initiative, Kally University, 2019.
- Hosted reading events around campus.
- Trained graduate students to work with undergraduate students on reading strategies.

PUBLICATIONS

Peer-reviewed Articles and Chapters

Alcero, Mia. "How Writing Centers Can Help Students with Research." *WC Writes*, 10 (9) 2019. 90-101.

Alcero, Mia. "First-year Writing Tutors Speak." *Writing Daily*, edited by Carol Sykes. Education Press, 2018.

Reviews

Alcero, Mia. Review of Writing Center Times. *WC Writes* 9(16) 2018. 34-39.

Works In Progress

Alcero, Mia. "Administrative Work: How Writing Centers Can Do Better." Under review with *Journal of Writing Center Research.*

Alcero, Mia and Chad Franks. *Letting Students Help Students*. Edited collection.

PRESENTATIONS AND WORKSHOPS

"Firsts for First-year Writing Students: Working to Help Them Grow as Writers." Conference on First-year Writing, 2022.

"How to Keep Track of Writing Center Data." Workshop Series for Writing Center Administrators, 2021.

"Making Training Accessible for All Tutors." Workshop Series for Writing Center Administrators, 2020.

"Using Workshopping Techniques While Tutoring." Conference for First-year Writing, 2019.

GRANTS AND AWARDS

Department of English Mini Grant, Holt University, 2021.
National Writing Center Fellows Grant, 2019.
Teacher of the Semester Award, Holt University 2019.

PROFESSIONAL AFFILIATIONS

Writing Center Administration Coalition (member since 2018).
First-year Composition Association (member since 2018).
Organization for English as a Profession (secretary 2018, member since 2017).

REFERENCES

Available upon request.

FIGURE A.2 (Continued)

In addition to working your way through the questions, you might try redesigning some of this CV. For instance, craft two versions of the service section and compare them. What do you notice about your design choices in both versions? What do you like best? What don't you like? In doing this comparing and contrasting, reflect on why you made the design choices you did. What can you learn from this experience that can help you design your own CV?

A.4 Reimagining a Teaching Philosophy

In addition to the CV in the previous activity (Section A.3), Mia Alcero created a teaching philosophy statement too (see below). Using reflection and rhetorical thinking, work through the following questions. These questions are meant to help you think about how and why faculty write teaching philosophy statements and what stories they tell. After working through these questions, make a plan for either writing your own teaching philosophy statement or revising one you have already written.

1. What are your first impressions of Mia's statement? What stories does this statement tell about Mia? You could do a story audit here; that is, you could identify what stories are present and what stories are missing.
2. Would the statement example work for you? That is, if you were to use a similar structure and organization as well as content, would you have a statement that works for you, or would you find this type of statement limiting?
3. What would you do differently and why?
4. How could you revise Mia's statement to better show she is someone who values research's connection to what happens in a classroom? Someone who values collaboration among students and teachers? Imagining different versions of this statement might help you to imagine different versions of your own statement.
5. Based on what you reflected on in this activity, how might you approach redesigning your own statement?

As an additional activity, try rewriting one of Mia's paragraphs in her teaching philosophy to highlight a different value or belief. Then, reflect on this experience. How does this new paragraph change the rest of the statement? What does it add, for instance? Does this new paragraph still belong in the same place, or do all the paragraphs in the statement now need to be reorganized?

And yet another activity, identify what Mia's statement silently assumes about education and about students. Exploring the implied messages in this text, determine whether you would either eliminate these or bring them into the foreground. If you choose to transition these assumptions into statements, how does that change the central ideas present?

Mia Alcero
Teaching Philosophy

Reading and discussing student writing is vital to a writing classroom in order for a community of writers to foster effective critical thinking and analysis techniques. Learning is an active process that requires both students and instructors working together to find relationships between studied material and experiences in life. A writing classroom that explores those connections is important to the development of writing skills. For instance, a classroom discussion of the rhetorical appeals of ethos, pathos, and logos can enable writers to critically analyze the texts they encounter in their daily lives whether those texts are books, websites, text messages, or digital articles. The goals of such a rhetorical discussion are 1) to help students formulate ways of critically examining texts and 2) to help them apply what they have learned to their own writing.

In order to keep the learning process engaging, I conduct a classroom that not only cultivates individual learning, but also collaborative learning. For example, participation in a group writing activity which asks students to draft a persuasive letter on a current issue allows for an exploration of many perspectives. At the same time, this activity asks students to formulate their own understanding of writing by first drawing on what others have to say and then by drawing on their own experiences. While each student describes their world differently, writers must find appropriate ways to help readers connect to their texts. The goals of this collaborative activity, therefore, are to help students expand their writing experiences to include others in the process and to develop new ways of looking at individual experiences from which we write about.

In my classroom, students and I read and study many texts, from social media posts to presidential speeches, that serve as models of what we can do as writers, as well as teach us about writing and how to use various writing strategies in diverse contexts. We also write in the writing classroom to put into practice what we learn from our readings, whether that is through brainstorming, outlining, or drafting. And, throughout the course, we discuss our writing with the goal of learning more about the connections between our life experiences and the writing we do.

FIGURE A.3 Teaching philosophy example.

This teaching philosophy illustrates a common document genre requested in many (US-based) academic job advertisements and performance review portfolios.

A.5 Designing Feedback for Student Work

In this activity, think about how you respond to your students' writing. While every discipline's assessment practices vary, most of us respond to student writing in some form or another. You may only see short samples of student writing in a discussion board or through an in-class activity, or you may work with longer products. Regardless of the length or purpose, identify one type of student writing you work with regularly and reflect on how you respond. To reflect, answer the following:

- Do you offer general feedback on the content and style of the writing?
- Do you focus on one thing, such as alignment with the assignment prompt or mechanics?

- Do you offer in-text feedback? Do you offer summative end comments?
- Does the student work and the assessment become a conversation?
- How much time does it take to respond?
- Do you respond in a particular modality (i.e., text, voice note, video, etc.)?

As you reflect on your answers, jot down some of the more poignant aspects of your response process. Then, identify one or two parts of your response process that you want to try approaching differently. For example, if you offer text-based feedback in the form of many in-text annotations, maybe you want to try writing students a letter that includes a few of the main points you'd normally raise in comments. Or, maybe you want to offer a voice note for students with spoken feedback they can listen to as they read through the product. You could pause here and do a comparison between your written feedback and your voice feedback, noting how they are different. As you spend time reflecting on how you can design feedback differently, consider whether that feedback will be usable and accessible to students. Remember that when we design, it is important that all our users can use and access our documents effectively.

As another activity, if you prefer, identify a type of student work that you frequently respond to that isn't writing. Maybe your students produce charts or video content, or maybe they paint or sculpt in your classes. Your courses may include spreadsheets of data or schematics. Choose one assignment or genre of student work that isn't writing and repeat this activity. Reflect on your response practices and identify one or two elements within that practice that you want to approach differently. How can you better design your feedback so that it is usable and accessible?

A.6 Writing an Email to a Student

As faculty, we spend a lot of time responding to student emails. In this activity, imagine you have two weeks remaining in a class and a student has emailed you to request an extra credit opportunity for your course. This student has already failed to turn in two major assignments during the semester and is failing the course as a result. In their email, the student explains that they were having a hard time adjusting to college life at the beginning of the semester and failed to turn in those assignments as a result. The student notes that they will likely lose their scholarship if they don't pass your class.

How do you craft a response that is at the same time in line with your institution's policies but compassionate? Brainstorm and then design a few different ways in which you could address the student's email. For example, you could design one version with a policy-forward tone of voice, one version that is in a more empathetic voice, and one that is somewhere in between. Compare these to one another, weighing what messages (explicit and implicit) they send to the student.

A.7 Writing a Letter of Recommendation

Imagine that you are asked to write a letter of recommendation on behalf of a student who is applying for graduate school. The student, who is majoring in literature and minoring in biology, wishes to enroll in an M.A. in Design program. This student has been successful in many of your literature classes and you have worked with this student as part of an organization on campus. The student provides their resume for your review as well as a list of their accomplishments. As you read them, you notice that they have worked in the rec center on campus, won two academic awards at your institution for leadership, and have volunteered with a few local community organizations that don't explicitly connect with the graduate work they want to do. After speaking with the student, you learn that their goals for attending the graduate program are to learn how to design stories and artwork for major publishers.

For this activity, write a sample letter following your general practices for recommendations. After you've completed the draft, take a moment to reflect on your approach for writing this letter. Make a few notes on your reflection that can help you revise. To help you get started, consider the following questions:

- What, if any, additional information from the student would have been helpful for writing the letter?
- Did you speak with anyone else (like other faculty who have worked with the student) before writing the letter?
- What kind of research, if any, into the program the student is applying to did you conduct?
- What kind of evidence did you or would you include in your recommendation letter?
- How did you draft your letter? Did you create an outline? Write particular paragraphs first? Did you revise it several times? Did you edit it several times?
- Did you ask a colleague to review your letter or a specific part of it? What kind of feedback were you seeking?

Next, take a few moments to identify what the audience needs in a recommendation letter and consider how you might meet those needs more effectively. Do you want to restructure your letter? Do you want to bold keywords, add subheadings, or include hyperlinks? Do you want to focus the letter on one theme, activity, or accomplishment?

Finally, draft a new iteration of your recommendation letter for this student. There are many ways to redesign a recommendation letter. You could write a thematic one, one that is based on skills, for example. So, you may find that you want to create a few different iterations of your draft and then compare them. In comparing them, you might ask: What stories am I telling with each version? And how do these stories prove the student is prepared for specific graduate study?

A.8 Creating Assignment Instructions

As instructors, we are responsible for creating assignments that help our students meet the learning outcomes for our courses. Writing effective instructions is crucial to our students' understanding. Yet, how do we write assignments that reach all our students when all our students have unique learning methods? For this activity, choose one of your existing assignments. Then, reimagine different versions of the design. For example, create a video of your instructions, an infographic, and a webpage. Next, consider novel approaches to broaden your perspective. Ask students what they think of the different versions. Ask your colleagues who don't teach your course what they think. Then, optimize creative thinking by experimenting with role-playing. Use GenAI to act like a student and have it complete the assignment. Finally, reflect on this experience, noting what was liberating in your approach and what was not.

A.9 Revising a Course Policy

At the beginning of a semester, we give our students a syllabus that outlines our expectations as well as our policies for the course. For this activity, choose one of your course's policies that you created and revise it using GOOD principles for divergent design. In other words, first, generate abundance. Consider as many possibilities for writing this policy as possible. Try different versions of the design. For example, use keywords or sections and subheadings.

Next, consider novel approaches to broaden your perspective. Ask students what they think of the different versions. Ask your colleagues who don't teach your course what they think.

Then, optimize creative thinking by experimenting with role-playing. Use GenAI to simulate different students (e.g., someone who is dyslexic and someone who speaks multiple languages) and have it read the policy and interpret it. What results do you get?

Likewise, discover the unexpected by challenging assumptions and answering "what if" questions about your policy. What if, for instance, your policy had a theme or focused on one word as its guiding thesis? Trying different ways of looking at your policy may help you realize the assumptions you have made about your students and the class.

Finally, test your new policy by asking a student to paraphrase it in their own words. In this kind of test, you are asking your student to share their understanding of your policy. If you find that your student's paraphrase is aligned with what you intended for the policy, then you were likely successful in how you communicated it. Then, ask your student what impression they have (i.e., what they feel) about the class as a result of the policy. It is one thing to know that our intention with our writing has been communicated effectively and yet another to know how our messages are welcomed.

For another activity, you could redesign the syllabus policy provided in Figure A.4. This policy is for students who turn in their work late and is listed under course policies on the syllabus along with all other policies for the course. As you work through this example, identify what assumptions it makes about students. How does it assume students will read this statement? Just as well, you might consider what this policy is missing.

Next, brainstorm as many possibilities for the policy using divergent practices. Then narrow these down using convergent practices. It is worth noting here that while content is important, you should also keep in mind the tone of the policy and how the policy is structured or organized. Draw on the work you did earlier in this book with information architecture to redesign it.

Policy for Turning in Late Work:
All due dates for assignments and activities are indicated on the syllabus to help you succeed in this class. All assignments are due before you come to class. Therefore, if you turn in your assignment during class, it will be counted late. If you miss a deadline, you are eligible to turn in the assignment up to four days late and earn up to 80% of the grade for that assignment. If you have a medical condition, have to attend a funeral, or have jury duty that prevents you from turning in assignments on time, you should speak with the office of Student Disability Services as soon as you can. Doctor's notes as well as other types of documents related to your absences should go to the Student Disability Services office only. Here is their website with contact info: www.studentdisability.edu. Please do not wait until the end of the semester to contact this office. You should do this immediately following your absence or inability to turn work in on time.

FIGURE A.4 Late work policy.

This example policy can be used to complete the activity.

A.10 Identifying Invisible Labor

This activity can help you find opportunities to advocate through design. Take a few moments and think about how you work, the steps you take to complete specific activities. You may find it helpful to look at some of your professional materials such as your CV, a course syllabus or assignment, a website you've developed, and so on. Then think about a few things you do that aren't included in these example materials you've collected. This labor could include problem-solving department issues, peer mentoring, advising work, and other similarly unseen work.

Once you've identified some of your professional activities as a focal point for this exercise, make a thorough list of labor needed to complete each activity. Note the steps or actions that are difficult to include in your professional documents. Inventory when, where, why, and how this labor is performed.

Take a moment to reflect on what you have listed. From here, you could work in a few different directions. You could reimagine your professional documents in ways that better represent this labor. Or, you could create a "shadow CV" that prioritizes this labor and submit it alongside your current materials. Or, you might map this work with the intention of presenting it to your administrators as an illustration of a particular challenge you face in your day-to-day work.

Reflect on how you can transform this information into valued content. You might look at the language the system supports, for instance, and find ways to ethically translate your invisible labor into it. You might ask colleagues to contribute to your document to create a more substantial overview of your community's labor. You might consider identifying a few small, concrete actions your institution could make to better recognize this work and advocate for these small changes.

A.11 Planning a Curriculum Proposal

Faculty design a number of curriculum-related documents, including curriculum proposals. This genre can include proposing updates to existing courses, programs, and procedures (i.e., policies, assessment, etc.), and developing new courses, programs, and procedures. In this activity, consider what it takes to design a successful proposal and develop a workflow for creating the document.

First, if you are currently working on a curriculum proposal, locate your draft (or if you don't have a draft yet, use your notes). If you are not currently working on a proposal, brainstorm some possible future curriculum changes that you would like to see implemented that would warrant a proposal.

Next, start with the whys: why this proposal and why now? Write your answers to these questions so that you can "see" what makes this moment the best time for your proposed ideas. In writing a proposal, faculty must justify their choices and provide readers with an adequate rationale that supports what is being proposed.

As a next step, make a list of stakeholders (i.e., students, faculty, administrators, staff, external reviewers) and identify what each stakeholder needs from the proposal. Identifying all the stakeholders involved in a curriculum proposal can be challenging and may require talking with colleagues and administrators to develop a thorough list.

Then, inventory the assumptions you are making with your proposal. It may be helpful to return to Table 6.1 in Chapter 6. Critically reflect on the voices that might be unintentionally left out or misrepresented. Then consider how you can design a better proposal that mitigates or eliminates the negative impact(s) of these assumptions.

In professional settings, we tend to learn through models. We may read a colleague's performance review portfolio to learn what reviewers expect in the cover letter, for example. Importantly, this kind of modeling not only shows us what others value, it also helps us identify what we value. As you develop your plan, examine past proposals. What do you notice about them? What do they have in common? What is missing? What stands out to you or surprises you? What worries you? Make notes as you review the model proposals you've selected and return to these often throughout the development process. Table 1.4 in Chapter 1 may be a helpful guide for organizing your thoughts.

Finally, develop your workflow. Write a short reflection that helps you plan your document and identifies key points of interest from your notes. The workflow can take whatever form is most useful to you. You may develop a map or an outline, a bulleted list in a memo, or even a series of sticky notes. Consider how your reflection can help guide content and design choices throughout the process. Make sure to account for both the steps needed to develop the proposal and the time needed to test and reflect on the design and content.

A.12 Redesigning a Dynamic Research Statement

Academic professionals use research statements for many reasons. We write statements for job and grant applications, annual performance reviews, promotion or sabbatical consideration, recognition, and so on. Importantly, we don't always have time to sit and write a research statement from scratch, and it can be helpful to have a dynamic, adaptable statement on hand that we can quickly revise to meet our immediate purpose.

For this activity, craft a basic research statement that can serve as a foundation for writing other research statements. This foundational statement will later be adapted for various audiences such as hiring committees, promotion review committees, and so forth.

Before drafting, however, make a list of "must haves." What must your foundational statement have and why? Reflect on your choices and determine why you made them. This can help you prioritize.

As another activity, you could use the following research statement from a history professor and redesign it for different audiences, such as for students, for faculty who are not in the same discipline, and for administrators reviewing a tenure application. To do so, you might start by identifying what impressions this statement gives and what stories it tells about the professor's research. You might think about what is missing. Then, you could imagine the different audiences this might be written for and their expectations in order to plan your redesign of the statement. Remember to view a research statement such as this as a foundation and one that is dynamic; that is, it should be succinct and adaptable in different forms for different audiences. After you reimagine the statement below, reflect on your design choices and why you made them.

Research Statement:

For the past ten years, the focus for my research has centered on the Indigenous histories, cultures, and identities of Central Plains tribes in America. The tribes' physical and spiritual connections to the land, its wildlife and fauna, serve as a means to study the integral ways in which humans care for and shape ecological systems over time. It also allows us to reflect on how traditions and generational knowledge endure and adapt. By shedding light on these connections, my research challenges the colonial and western narratives that overshadow Indigenous voices.

Through archival work, interviews, and field studies, I have studied the region extensively, giving voice to contemporaries with the goal of bridging the past with the present. The purpose of my research is to preserve and to advocate for place-based histories and traditions by acknowledging the deep relationships tribes have with their land. In addition to publishing a book about my experiences documenting tribal life, my scholarship has been published in peer-reviewed journals and I have presented at several major conferences. I see my research as an ongoing scholarly conversation and exploration on people's understanding and respect for the land that sustains them.

FIGURE A.5 Research statement.

This example provides a research statement you can use to complete this activity.

A.13 Research One-Pager

The research one-pager is a useful document for any project and may be a required part of a funding application or a performance review. One-pagers often provide a brief summary of a research project that focuses on the project's implications for an audience or population and its role in a larger scholarly conversation or pursuit. Frequently, this document will include significant findings if the project is in an advanced state. Importantly, a one-pager should be designed as an at-a-glance overview of the project (or the idea for a project) and should offer stakeholders key information they need to understand the work and any request accompanying the document.

For this activity, choose a research project you haven't written a one-pager for and brainstorm a list of information you should include about it in a one-pager. Next, brainstorm some possible ways in which to organize

Land as Cultural Relationship: Central Plains Tribes and the Stewardship of Place

Core Goals

Foregrounding Indigenous voices, this research project aims to preserve the spiritual and cultural traditions of the Central Plain tribes with the goal of challenging colonial narratives that have disrupted the relationships these tribes have had with the land that sustains them. The study's purpose is to provide a voice for the tribes and a unique perspective on the interconnections Indigenous people have with land, wildlife, and fauna in an evolving ecological system.

Methodology

This study employs a mixed-method research approach that integrates the analysis of government ddocuments (i.e., treaties, recordings of oral histories, and maps) with ethnographic archival accounts of Central Plains tribes. In addition, it relies on a six-month field study conducted in the Platte River in Nebraska and the historic homeland of the Pawnee Nation of Oklahoma. The interviews, observations, and artifact analysis conducted at these sites provided additional key insights into the deeply rooted and rich traditions of a culture connected to its land.

Results

The results of this study show that the Central Plains Tribes, their histories, cultures, and traditions are fundamentally intertwined with land itself. It is their identity. The interviews and oral histories demonstrate how evolving generational understandings of this connection have changed due to colonial ideologies and reveal how governments, political, economic forces, put pressure on the land and therefore the people that are connected to it.

Outcomes

This research project's results were adapted into a monograph and conference presentation that advocates for preserving Central Plains Tribes' traditional connections with land. This study has been integrated in a grant application to support the development of an educational center that will contribute to and help sustain the generational knowledge of the Central Plains Tribes.

Next Steps

Because this is an ongoing attempt for preservation, the next phase of this research will involve a community partnership mapping project. Using oral histories, this phase will attempt to redraw ancestral lands and reclaim connections with those lands.

FIGURE A.6 Research one-pager example.

This example illustrates pertinent content to include in a one-pager and uses a conventional organizational structure.

and present this information. Think about the design choices you will need to make when doing so. Finally, draft your one-pager and share it with a colleague for feedback. Ask your colleague to think aloud as they engage with it so that you can take notes. Use these notes to revise and as you revise, try justifying each of your design choices.

A.14 Using Information Architecture

The assignment instructions in Figure A.7 lack a purposeful information architecture. Redesign these instructions so that they follow the principles presented in Chapter 3. Then, reflect on your experience.

For context, the assignment is for an undergraduate Introduction to Sociology course at a small urban community college. Students are learning how to identify and define the social forces that shape communities and the individuals who reside in them. They are discussing concepts of power and inequality as they relate to societies. This example may at first seem over-the-top in its design. But such an example demonstrates how each design choice we make must be thoughtful and justified.

Assignment instructions: Three-page essay: describe a social institution* and explain how broader social forces** shape it. Sociology is the study of human's social behaviors, specifically the patterns that arise, as these behaviors shape and are shaped by: cultures, institutions, politics, race, class, gender	**Typed-essay** **12-point font**
It examines the inequalities and power dynamics that arise and the control that is afforded some, and is excluded from others. Must do: provide examples that help to explain and demonstrate your main argument, must have a clear introduction and conclusion, and must cite all your sources when including information that is not your own. *(such as education or healthcare) **(such as class, gender, race) **Please note that AI should not be used to write this essay.**	Note: Turn this in on February 8 via our course management system where you will find grading criteria

FIGURE A.7 Assignment prompt example.

This example illustrates assignment instructions that do not follow the principles of information architecture.

A.15 Develop a Decision–Revision Journal

This activity asks you to track your decisions and actions as you develop documents. The title, "Decision–Revision Journal," implies core tenets we've learned in this book: design is a series of choices and revision permeates design. This log can help you identify the intentionality in your document design and leverage it more effectively as you develop your design practices. Importantly, this activity is ongoing and can facilitate a generative space for you to explore, analyze, and understand your design and writing processes.

To get started, choose a space in which you will maintain your journal or action log. Consider what kind of information you will want to include and how you want to access it. If you are prone to journal writing, you may want to use a word processing application like Microsoft Word or Pages. If you want more of a snapshot view of your activities, you may want a spreadsheet application like Google Sheets. If you prefer more visual tracking, developing a space in Canva or Prezi could prove useful.

Then establish a few categories of actions and related information you want to track. To help you identify criteria, consider your strengths and your challenges, or reflect on a specific document you recently developed. Do you want to better understand the choices you make during the early stages of a project? Do you want to track specific design elements you use? Do you think you need more time for iterations? Do you want to share your drafts more frequently throughout your process or design for more complex user engagement?

Then, choose a document that you recently designed that needs to be revised—a document that's still in development. If you used a document like this to help you establish your journal's structure, use it for this first entry. Before you begin revising, take a moment and reflect on the decisions that you made and why you made them. Log these so that you have a record of them. Next, begin your revisions and take a few moments here and there to make notes in your journal. Consider the choices you're making, your rationale for revising (or not revising), and the impact of these choices.

Tracking decisions and revisions over time and across drafts can help you better understand your design process and reflect on what is working and what isn't. It also gives you a chance to identify constraints and challenges, plan ways to overcome them, and assess your success.

A.16 Design Technologies

For this activity, reflect on your use of design technologies. After completing one of the activities above, make a list of the technologies you used to complete it and then answer the following questions:

1 Why did you choose to use those technologies?
2 Were there other technologies you could have used, and if so, why didn't you?
3 What affordances and constraints did those technologies have, and how did you navigate them?
4. If you could rework your document, would you rely on other technologies? Why or why not?

Our choice in technology is rhetorical and should not be one of convenience. Indeed, if we want to ensure our designs are usable and accessible, then how we design and with what technologies must be justified through rhetorical thinking.

Try redesigning one of the documents you created in an earlier activity using a different technology. Consider how this technology led you to different design decisions. For example, if you created a research statement using Microsoft Word, try designing your research statement again in Microsoft PowerPoint. What changes for your statement when you do this, and why? How does a different technology make you think differently about this statement? Do you have to organize it differently? Do you have to make different decisions about font sizes?

Reflecting on the design choices we make with different technologies can lead us to additional opportunities for serving our own needs as well as others.

APPENDIX B

Glossary

This glossary includes brief definitions of the important terms in this book. Defining words can be a tricky endeavor as they are shaped by social, cultural, racial, and gendered histories. Context shapes meaning as well as the connotations that words carry with them. Some words in this glossary are more abstract than others, and some have nuanced meanings dependent on the (cultural or disciplinary) application, which makes defining them accurately and thoroughly difficult. For these reasons, this glossary should serve as a starting point, not an ending. We encourage you to pursue other definitions as well as question those we have provided below.

Accessibility The extent to which a document removes obstacles so that people with diverse abilities and needs can interact and understand it.

Affordance All the possible ways in which a document, technology, or artifact enables a user to act.

AI Artificial intelligence. Any technology that performs human tasks by learning from data, analyzing human input, and then generating outputs that are based on probabilities.

AI collaborator A function that allows users to personalize and train an AI technology to take on a particular persona for a particular purpose and context. This can be achieved through setting parameters and can enhance the usefulness of the AI technology to better serve the needs of its users.

AI output The material received from a prompt provided to a GenAI.

Architecture The art and science of designing meaningful structures, spaces, and systems for all who use them by taking into account the convergence of tools, processes, techniques, and people.

Arrangement (rhetorical canon) A rhetorical approach for organizing and structuring ideas in specific ways to best help communicate a document's messages.

Assemblages A theoretical and practical approach of bringing together people, environments, media, and/or technologies in ways that challenge traditional constructs or representations.

Assessment The process for determining a design's usability and accessibility through reflection and testing. This often involves collecting and interpreting information about users' experiences interacting with a design as well as acknowledging our stories, our users' stories, and our documents' stories.

Brainstorm Creative idea generation; imagining possibilities for designing a document.

Clarity The opposite of conveying misunderstanding; providing quality things (such as ideas, structures, elements, and sentences) in documents that can be quickly read and understood.

Constraint The boundaries and restrictions that establish a design's possibilities. These are often informed by a design's related convention, such as genre, media, culture, or technology.

Convergence A method of design in which analysis of the intersections within the rhetorical situation guides design choice(s).

Convergent design A strategy that focuses on the most effective pathway in shaping, evaluating, revising, and polishing ideas for distribution.

CORE principles A convergent framework for designing documents through categorizing ideas, ordering them, refining them, and then enacting them into a final draft.

Counterstory A meaning-making approach that prioritizes marginalized experiences and silenced voices. A narrative resistance to hegemonic values and priorities.

Craft The rhetorical act of making that involves both humans and nonhumans and emphasizes the materials we use to design and how those are controlled.

Data storytelling Using narratives created by data to communicate the value and purpose of the information.

Define (the problem) To thoroughly specify and depict the parts making up a design problem, usually started at the beginning of the design process.

Design To create meaningfully by effectively utilizing rhetorical reflection, design thinking, technology use, and information architecture.

Design justice Actively ensuring that designs serve underrepresented users.

Design thinking The ability to problem-solve documents by centering complex human experiences.

Divergence A method encouraging an abundance of ideas and approaches in response to a specific problem.

Divergent design Utilizing lateral thinking, this is an inventive strategy for designing documents that prioritizes generating an abundance of innovative and novel approaches to find creative solutions.

Documents The various kinds of products we create, circulate, and consume; includes page- and screen-based texts, sensory-specific texts, and living texts.

Empathize Strongly considering a document's audiences and their unique needs, then using this knowledge to design texts that are responsive.

Findability The extent to which users can easily locate what they are looking for in a document in a reasonable amount of time.

Flexibility The extent to which a document can be adapted for the changing needs of diverse users and contexts. This also can refer to how well a document can accommodate its users over time.

GenAI Generative artificial intelligence. AI technologies that can produce new text, images, audio, video, or code.

Genre conventions Common or reoccurring document features that indicate to users what type of document they are using. Features could include specific structures, language, and content that are used in a particular type of text regularly.

GOOD principles A divergent framework for designing documents through generating abundance, originating novel approaches, optimizing creative thinking, and discovering the unexpected.

Human in the loop (HITL) A method for working with AI that recognizes that, in order for AI technologies' output to be ethically and effectively leveraged in a product, humans must be an integral part of the production process.

Human work strategy A methodology prioritizing human engagement and contribution.

Ideation The act of creatively thinking about all possibilities for a design problem.

Inclusive design An intentional approach to designing documents that takes into consideration all users and their unique needs, circumstances, and abilities.

Information architecture The accessible design of communication for/in particular contexts for specific audiences. The strategic utilization of rhetoric to build a careful organization and arrangement of a communication's elements.

Integration A method for combining elements of a rhetorical situation with tools and technologies to build a document so that its parts cohesively work together to meet the needs of users. The ability for information, technologies, and tools to connect with one another to support a clear meaning.

Invention (rhetorical canon) A rhetorical approach for discovering ideas that considers purpose, audience, genre, and context.

Iteration The development of new, more creative drafts that capitalize on envisioning better versions of previous drafts. The goal of iteration is to discover possibilities.

Labeling A strategy for identifying and naming parts or terms of a document so that they can be organized as well as recognized. This is used to describe not only the content but also the features and functions of a document.

Lateral thinking Prioritizing unconventional, creative problem-solving.

Linear thinking Prioritizing logical, systematic problem-solving.

LLMs Large Language Models. AI technologies capable of producing language outputs that resemble human responses because they have been trained on vast datasets of human language.

Multimodality A coming together of multiple modes to make purposeful meaning.

Navigation A method for organizing a document so that users can move from one part or element seamlessly to the next. In using things like headings, links, and menus, it provides pathways that help users find their way through the content.

Organization A strategy for arranging content in a document, including information, in a clear, logical manner so that it is straightforwardly navigable and understood. Plays an integral role in information architecture.

Point-of-view (PoV) statements A reflection or position that takes into consideration the perspective of users (and their needs) in relation to the problem or purpose of the design process.

Post-process theory A framework that posits the connectedness of writing, and the act of writing, to its cultural and political contexts.

Prototype Developing a version of a document that can be tested with users with the goal to revise based on the test's outcomes.

Recursive revision A process that involves making changes throughout the development of a document by rereading, rethinking, and reshaping. Often a nonlinear process that involves returning to previously developed ideas or content before advancing further in the development process.

Reflection A thinking process focusing on analyzing an experience in order to learn from it.

Responsive revision A rhetorical act that considers what users value when experiencing a document in a particular context and revising strategically to better meet those needs. A process for making adjustments to a document based on user feedback.

Revision Iterative process for reshaping ideas.

Rhetorical canons A classical framework rooted in the history of rhetoric. It provides a means for effectively thinking through the communicative process, from initial idea to the delivery of that idea to its audience.

RICE method An approach for evaluating an idea that calculates reach, impact, confidence, and effort.

Scalability The ability to expand and grow without sacrificing the effectiveness and accessibility of a document.

Story A historically, culturally, and socially constructed process for meaning making that is layered with the intersections of designers, users, and contexts.

Testing An iterative step in design thinking that evaluates whether a design will work with its intended audience. Designers note what works and what does not with the goal of refining iterations based on feedback.

Transformative design Design creation and implementation actions that prioritize creating equitable, sustainable, inclusive designs or systems of design.

Usability The extent to which a text can be easily and efficiently accessed and understood as well as the extent to which it meets users' needs and their ability to navigate information.

User A human and/or nonhuman that will utilize your document to meet their/its needs.

User experience (UX) Defines the overall interactive experiences that a user has when utilizing a document.

Wicked problems Entangled problems that require the exploration of multiple pathways to find creative and often alternative nonlinear solutions.

INDEX

Pages in *italics* refer to figures and pages in **bold** refer to tables.

For Product Safety Concerns and Information please contact our EU
representative GPSR@taylorandfrancis.com
Taylor & Francis Verlag GmbH, Kaufingerstraße 24, 80331 München, Germany

www.ingramcontent.com/pod-product-compliance
Ingram Content Group UK Ltd.
Pitfield, Milton Keynes, MK11 3LW, UK
UKHW022354190926
475702UK00015B/2290

9781041206163

PUBLIC RELATIONS AND STRATEGIC COMMUNICATION IN 2050

Taking stock of the technological, political, economic, and social trends that exist today, this book extends the discussion to analyze and predict how these trends will affect the public relations and strategic communication industry of the future.

This book is divided into two sections, the first addressing such key topics as artificial intelligence (AI), big data, political polarization, and misinformation, the second looking at key facets of the profession, such as media relations, crisis communication, and measurement and evaluation. Leading researchers in the discipline share their analysis of these topics while also providing theoretically based and practically relevant insights on how the industry must evolve to keep up with, and perhaps anticipate, changes in culture, society, and technology.

This book will be of interest to scholars, industry professionals, and advanced undergraduate and graduate students in public relations and strategic communication.

Alexander V. Laskin is a Professor of Advertising and Public Relations at Quinnipiac University, USA.

Karen Freberg is a Professor in Strategic Communications at the University of Louisville, USA.